PUNCTUATION FOR NOW

A 'Colon' from *Punctuation Personified or Pointing Made Easy by Mr Stops*, 1824

(from a private collection; photograph provided by the Victoria and Albert Museum)

Punctuation for Now

John McDermott

MACMILLAN

First published 1990

Published by
THE MACMILLAN PRESS LTD
Houndmills, Basingstoke, Hampshire RG21 2XS
and London
Companies and representatives
throughout the world

Typeset by Wessex Typesetters
(Division of The Eastern Press Limited)
Frome, Somerset

Printed in Hong Kong

British Library Cataloguing in Publication Data
McDermott, John, *1948–*
Punctuation for now.
1. English language. Punctuation
I. Title
421
ISBN 0–333–51067–4 (hard cover)
ISBN 0–333–51068–2 (paperback)

In memory of

DACRE BROWN

Praising what is lost
Makes the remembrance dear

Contents

Starting Points

No levell'd malice
Infects one comma in the course I hold . . . .
Shakespeare, *Timon of Athens*, i.i.46–7

As peace should still her wheaten garland wear
And stand a comma 'tween their amities . . . .
Shakespeare, *Hamlet*, v.ii.40–1

All the parts of Syntaxe have already beene declared. There resteth one generall affection of the whole, disposed thorow every member thereof, as the blood is thorow the body; and consisteth in the breathing, when we pronounce any *Sentence* . . . .

The English Grammar Made by Ben Jonson
(c. 1617, published 1640)

Points, serving for the better Understanding of Words, are either *Primary*, or *Secondary*.

Primary Points, which shew their Tone, Sound and Pauses, are eight: four simple and more common; Period, [.] Colon, [:] Semi-colon, [;] Comma [,] and four mixt and less frequent. . . .

The mixt Points, are *Erotesis* [?] *Ecphonesis*; [!] *Parenthesis*, ( ) *Parathesis*: [ ] which have always some simple Point, exprest or understood, in them. . . .

Secondary Points, now shewing Tone, Sound, or Pause are *four*: Apostrophus ['] Eclipsis, [—] or [– –] Dieresis, [..] and Hyphen, [-] or ["].

Charles Butler, *The English Grammar* (1633)

Great care ought to be had in writing, for the due observing of points: for, the neglect thereof will pervert the sence.

Richard Hodges, *The English Primrose* (1644)

Pointing is the disposal of speech into certain members for more articulate and distinct reading and circumstantiating of writs and papers. It rests wholly and solely on concordance, and necessitates a knowledge of grammar.

Robert Monteith,
The True and Genuine Art of Pointing (1704)

I know, there are some *persons* who affect to *despise* it, and treat this whole Subject with the utmost *Contempt*, as a Trifle far below their Notice, and a Formality unworthy of *their* Regard: They do not hold it difficult, but *despicable*; and neglect it, as being *above* it.

Yet many learned Men have been highly sensible of its Use; and some ingenious and elegant Writers have condescended to point their Works with Care; and very eminent Scholars have not disdained to teach the Method of doing it with Propriety.

James Burrow,
An Essay on the Use of Pointing (1771)

It has already been frequently shown by writers on the subject that our punctuation-marks do not indicate the most suitable places for pauses in reading aloud; the voice of an intelligent reader ignores some of the textual pointing and introduces breaks at places other than those where there are points. The pointing of matter 'to be sung or said' is, in fact, a subject apart. With regard to constructional pointing it may be urged that in reality it rests on sense and meaning, since grammar is the analysis of the forms in which rational expression is made. We think, however, that all the complexities and divergences and confusions of grammatical pointing arose just because it was not in constant and direct touch with meaning.

A Practical Printer, *A Manual of Punctuation* (1859)

Modern printers make an effort to be guided by logic or grammar alone; it is impossible for them to succeed entirely; but any one who will look at an Elizabethan book with the original stopping will see how far they have moved: the old stopping was frankly to guide the voice in reading aloud, while the modern is mainly to guide the mind in seeing through the grammatical construction.

H. W. and F. G. Fowler, *The King's English* (1906)

When punctuation was first employed, it was in the role of the handmaid of prose; later the hand-maid was transformed by the pedants into a harsh-faced chaperone, pervertedly ingenious in the contriving of stiff regulations and starched rules of decorum; now, happily, she is content to act as an auxiliary to the writer and as a guide to the reader.

Harold Herd,
Everybody's Guide to Punctuation (1925)

. . . to treat our system of punctuation, not as an art to be taught, but as an established fact, as a human institution of considerable interest that merits scientific examination.

Reginald Skelton,
Modern English Punctuation (1933)

Most people would agree that punctuation is a matter not only of rules but of personal taste. . . . I should define [it] as being governed two-thirds by rule and one-third by personal taste.

G. V. Carey, *Mind the Stop* (1939)

We indicate time by means of stops known as punctuation marks. These marks also help to make the sense clear, to show the expression, and to avoid confusion in reading.

L. A. G. Strong,
An Informal Grammar of English (1943)

For really bad punctuation there is no excuse save fear.

Basil Cottle, *The Plight of English* (1975)

Lastly, it ought to be added that in one or two cases a particular way of spelling a word or punctuating a sentence has been completely changed. This does not often mean that an error has been discovered in the 'Rules'; but rather that the fashion has altered . . . .

Horace Hart, Preface (1913),
Hart's Rules for Compositors and Readers at the University Press Oxford, 39th edn (1983)

Attainment targets at age 7: . . .

3   Write simple sentences, using full stops, capital letters and commas, word spacing . . . .

Kingman Committee of Inquiry into the Teaching of English Language (1988)

Preface

Ther is so greet diversite
In English, and in wrytyng of oure tonge,
So prey I God that non miswryte thee . . . .
Chaucer, *Troilus and Criseyde*,
v.1793–5

The title *Punctuation for Now* indicates both an intention and a belief. The intention is to survey the current best practice in the use of punctuation by educated writers of English. In this sense it is aimed at those people who received their formal education at a time when it was thought anathema to stifle children's inherent creativity (as it might be) by imposing upon them the elitist and inhibiting (let's say) and (probably) irrelevant structures of punctuation, which, in this respect, went the way of spelling and an attention to the structures of language, with the latter of which punctuation is

so intimately bound up. Many of those people –
and there is no reason to suppose that there is a
smaller proportion of bright, intelligent youngsters
in one generation than in another – are now of an
age where their talents and careers have brought
them to positions of influence (in teaching, publishing, journalism) where the more enlightened have
become aware of a shortage in the repertoire of
their skills. This book is written for these dis-
inherited, and at the request of some of them. It is
written also for those, older or more fortunate, to
whom the ideas of language as a system and
writing as an activity with rules were presented
from an early age. For them, for us, it is the case
that some of the rules governing the activity have
changed – not always for the worse – under a
variety of pressures. Here is the belief that underlies
my title. A look at earlier manuals of punctuation
(and at the clutch of preceding epigraphs) offers the
salutary warning that this aspect of our language
stands still no more than does vocabulary. The
language changes, grows, moves forward. That
many recent changes have been deplorable, viewed
in terms of either sense or beauty, is beyond
dispute; in particular the drift towards redundant
synonymy in merging, say, *uninterested* and *disin-
terested* is not just lazy but an impoverishment of
the language's capacity for nuance. At the same
time, though publishers and editors who care more
for the look of a page than its content have a lot to
answer for, there has been a tendency to streamline

received systems of punctuation that has, *on the whole*, been for the better. This aspect of our writing habits is undergoing a process of change; what is given here by way of guidance or instruction is necessarily provisional, an interim measure. The evidence of earlier handbooks is that we cannot hope to pin the system down like a butterfly for our collection.

This is far from saying that anything goes. The principles that have always governed good writing have not changed, but ways of working to those principles have; this explains the presence of the historical introduction that precedes the survey of usage. The survey does not blush to be prescriptive. It is part of the point of what I have to say that punctuation can be a very subtle instrument, and it is an area where (informed) taste is entitled to a say. However, to have argued all the *pro*s and *con*s would have used more space than was available, and, faced with choices, a writer must in the end decide to do *something*. If the prescriptions seem unnecessarily brusque at times, this is the reason, but I have tried wherever possible to call as evidence for the defence the practice of writers whose skill with the language is beyond question.

The book's purpose is primarily to give information. Thus, there is an opening section on the history of punctuation and of the derivation of the punctuation marks we use. An account of how they have been used in the past leads inevitably to matters of modern usage, where the aim has been to offer clear, firm guidance that accords with the best contemporary practice of educated, mature users of the language. At the end of some chapters, and in all of Chapters 5 and 6, there are examples of punctuation in use – sometimes very skilful use, sometimes historical, and sometimes a warning to the unwary.

The book will have served its purpose if those to whom punctuation is something of a mystery begin to apply its lessons to their own writing and to be more critically aware of its use in the books and newspapers they read.

Acknowledgements

Like any writer on punctuation, I am deeply indebted to some outstanding predecessors – notably Carey, the Fowlers and the Husbands, Partridge, Skelton and Vallins; the present work respectfully up-dates, rather than corrects, their achievements. The passages used in 'Historical Instances' are based on those given in Skelton's *Modern English Punctuation* (1933). For abundant help and advice on a wide range of matters I am obliged to Graham Eyre. Tim Farmiloe and Sarah Roberts-West have shown me great hospitality and encouragement on behalf of the publishers, and Tony Hilton helped with proofs. Not for the first time, I have benefited greatly from the unfailing friendliness, courtesy and efficiency of the staff of Wigan Reference Library.

As always, Anne has been – at all points – the best help imaginable.

1

Points to Note

---

*The sense or meaning of the words is very much
dependent upon the points which are used along with
the words.*

William Cobbett, *A Grammar of the English
Language* (1819)

WHAT IS PUNCTUATION?

Writing (nowadays at least) is marks made on
paper. These marks, whether made by hand or by
machine, differ from other such marks – those in
drawing, for example – by conveying a meaning
through words. And yet, left entirely to themselves, the words would not convey a great deal.

Consider, for instance,

WHATNOWMYLOVE

There are four words here, but if they are to make any sense they must be separated: WHAT NOW MY LOVE. Our first observation, then, needs to be that words alone are not enough to convey meaning, that – in print, certainly – there needs to be something *between* the words (in this case, spaces), or the product is nonsense, or non-sense. No spaces – no meaning. (In fact, there are languages – Japanese and Thai, for example – that do not use spaces in this way, though readers and writers do perceive individual words. Similarly, in these and other languages the European convention of reading from top to bottom and from left to right is supplanted by other conventions, recalling Swift's observation in *Gulliver's Travels*: 'but their manner of writing is very peculiar, being neither from the left to the right, like the Europeans; nor from the right to the left, like the Arabians; nor from up to down, like the Chinese; nor from down to up, like the Cascagians, but aslant from one corner of the paper to the other, like ladies in England'.) An English sentence is to this extent like a thimble, a sieve, a toasting-fork, or what you will. . . . Even so, we have not finished.

Having established some spaces in our earlier example, we are left with WHAT NOW MY LOVE. This is clearly progress, if only as something more convenient to deal with. But clearly it cannot remain like this. What else we introduce between the words – how we *punctuate* them, that is to say – can make a world of difference. Familiarity with a song of this title suggests *What now, my love?* The introduction, not just of spaces but of particular other marks (in this case a comma, a question mark and lower-case letters) makes sense of what had originally been no more than a string of letters at best cryptic, at worst meaningless.

Meaning, then, is imparted by what comes between the words. *What now, my love?* is now an acceptable sentence, as well as a fine song. But change what you put between the words, and you change what you get. See what an extra comma can do: *What,* now, *my love?* (Note too the reversal of the usual relations of italic and roman.) The effect is quite different; and different again if you replace the question mark with an exclamation mark and introduce some capitals: *What,* NOW, *my love!*

Popular songs are particularly vulnerable to this kind of change (compare 'What is this thing called "love"?' and 'What is this thing called, love?', or even 'What is *this* thing called, love?'). To show that this sort of thing is not confined to popular music, I recall a particularly zealous fellow student of mine (he was also doing Drama) who, in reading – of all things – Marlowe's *Edward II*, gave the line 'What would you with the King?' unduly theatrical pauses and emphases that would have to be transcribed as: 'What! would you? . . . with the *King*?'

Again, a notoriously philistine acquaintance re-routed W. H. Davies's lines from 'Leisure'

> What is this life, if, full of care,
> We have no time to stand and stare

to the much more vigorous

> What is this life if full of care?
> (*accelerando*) We have no time to stand and stare!

It is punctuation that makes sense of the chestnut enjoyed by generations of schoolboys: 'Charles I walked and talked half an hour after his head was cut off.' Again it is punctuation that makes intelligible the virtuoso (if rather pointless) feat of using the word *had* eleven times in succession: 'Louise, where Julia had had "had had", had had "had"; "had had" had had the teacher's approval'. And the painter who re-did the sign outside the Dog and Duck was berated by the landlord in these terms: 'there should be equal spaces between "Dog" and "and" and "and" and "Duck"'.

The non-sense or ambiguity that can result from mistaken or no punctuation has been exploited for serious literary effect. Shakespeare's play-within-a-play in *A Midsummer Night's Dream* owes much of its charm to Quince's putting in more stops than he pulls out:

> If we offend, it is with our good will.
> That you should think, we come not to offend,
> But with good will. To show our simple skill,
> That is the beginning of our end . . . .
>   *A Midsummer Night's Dream*, v.i.108–11

To return to *Edward II*, the message that goes to the deposed king's gaolers is carefully left unpointed to throw off suspicion:

> This letter, written by a friend of ours,
> Contains his death yet bids them save his life.
> *'Edwardum occidere nolite timere, bonum est'*;
> Fear not to kill the king, 'tis good he die.
> But read it thus, and there's another sense:
> *'Edwardum occidere nolite, timere bonum est'*;
> Kill not the king, 'tis good to fear the worst.
> Unpointed as it is, thus shall it go . . . .
>   Christopher Marlowe, *Edward II*, v.iv.6–13

(The fact that the transition in this message from Latin to English causes problems is a reminder that an inflected language such as Latin, in which most words vary their form to some extent according to their function and meaning, needs punctuation far less than an uninflected language such as English.)

Errors such as those noted above should keep us alert to the fact that the transmission of meaning by pauses and other signals is not restricted to writing but is central to speech also. The non-verbal components in a spoken exchange are sometimes called *paralinguistic*, and may be considered as either vocal or non-vocal. The vocal signals include such activities as yawning, shouting, whispering, or mimicking other speakers – all of which superimpose on the words an additional level of meaning, or, better, weave extra strands of significance into them. Non-vocal signals include nodding (in encouragement or agreement or reassurance of continuing attention), pursing of lips or eyebrows, smiling, scowling, and so on. John Lyons in his *Semantics* (1977) points out that these paralinguistic phenomena in conversation depend also on what he calls *modulation* and *punctuation*. Modulation he defines as 'the superimposing upon the utterance of a particular attitudinal colouring, indicative of the speaker's involvement in what he is saying and his desire to impress or convince the hearer'; punctuation is 'the marking of boundaries at the beginning and end of an utterance and at various points within the utterance to emphasize particular expressions, to segment the utterance into manageable information units, to solicit the listener's permission for the utterance to be continued, and so on'. Dickens makes a similar point a little more vividly in *Little Dorrit*:

'Indeed I have little doubt,' said Flora, running on with astonishing speed, and pointing her conversation with nothing but commas, and very few of them . . . .

Little Dorrit (1855–7) ch. 13

Under this heading *um*-ing and *er*-ing and *well*-ing buy time for the speaker to think out what he is saying and ask the hearer to be patient before butting in. We shall see later that written punctuation used at the highest levels of sophistication can work as effectively on paper as any of these paralinguistic features of speech.

This introduction has already used twenty or so different items of punctuation, so we are now in a position to attempt a definition and to see where it originates. Punctuation, then, is the use of spacing, conventional signs and certain typographical devices to promote understanding and to guide correct reading, whether silent or aloud. The word comes from Latin *punctus* or 'point', and from the fifteenth century to the beginning of the eighteenth the activity was called 'pointing'; the term punctuation, first recorded from the mid-sixteenth century, was initially used only of the insertion of vowel points in Hebrew texts (that is, the placing of marks next to consonants to indicate a vowel at that point). Sometime between 1650 and 1750 the two words exchanged meanings.

HISTORY[1]

The earliest remains, on pots and vases and memorials, show writing uninterrupted by spaces or marks. The punctuation system now used in English and other Western European languages has its origins in the practices of classical Greece and

Rome. Even so, there are some Greek inscriptions
from as early as the fifth century BC which show
phrases divided from each other by a vertical
string of two or three dots. Aristotle mentions the
paragraphos shown in some fourth-century literary
texts written on papyrus; this was a horizontal line
written under the first words of a new topic.
Euripides used a side-on *V* to indicate changes of
speaker in his *Antiope*. Aristophanes of Byzantium,
librarian at Byzantium in about 200 BC, is traditionally credited with the development of the critical
signs, marks of quantity, accents and breathings
still used in Greek script. His system, based on
rhetorical rather than grammatical principles,
divided texts into sections of different lengths. The
end of a short section (or *comma*) was marked by a
point after the middle of its last letter; that of a
longer section (*colon*) by a point placed after the
bottom of the last letter, and that of the longest
section (*periodos*) by one after the top. Such a
system, difficult to imagine in modern texts, was
helped to efficiency by the fact that books were still
written in majuscules, or the equivalent of modern
capital letters, which gave prominence to marks
that would have become lost in a welter of script
if the Greeks had invented joined-up writing. The
system was not often used in this form, and was
extended about the eighth century AD by the
addition of the question mark, which in Greek
practice resembles our semi-colon. (The modern
system of punctuating Greek texts is the work of

Renaissance printers in Italy and France, and their practice was built into the Greek types cut by Claude Garamond for Francis I of France between 1540 and 1550. Greek does not use a colon, and what we would call a semi-colon is marked by a high point. Quotation and exclamation marks are more recent additions.)

One of the most remarkable early Greek inscriptions is the twelve-columned record (now in the Louvre) found in the wall of a mill at Gortyn. This is written alternately from right to left and left to right, the columns succeeding each other from right to left. It is a legal document relating to fines, divorce, laws of succession and other domestic matters. There is no word separation at all, but in one of the columns a sign, as of two triangles laid horizontally with their apices pointing to each other, is placed between two clauses. There are isolated instances where an upright line is used to separate words, whilst in the sixth-century Sigeion marble (now in the British Museum) dots are used for division, usually in groups of two or three.[2]

By contrast, almost all Roman inscriptions show the use of points. In the oldest texts, from the end of the first century BC to the beginning of the second century AD, the points were used to divide words from each other. The introduction of a new topic was sometimes indicated by a type of paragraphing in which the first word or two of the new paragraph stood out into the margin (the current, contrary practice of indenting the first word has been standard since the seventeenth century). Roman scholars, among them the fourth-century grammarian Donatus and the sixth-century patron of monastic learning Cassiodorus, favoured Aristophanes' three-point system. The prevailing practice then, however, was to write continuously, the point between words having been abandoned. If the ends of sentences were marked at all, it was by a gap (sometimes followed by an enlarged letter) or very occasionally by a point.

The only significant development at this time was made by St Jerome (*c*.340–420). To promote the effective reading of liturgical texts and of the Vulgate, his translation of the Bible, Jerome devised a system of punctuation *per cola et commata* (i.e. by phrases). As its name and purpose suggest, this was a rhetorical system based on the manuscripts of orators, notably Demosthenes and Cicero. Each phrase began with a letter projecting into the margin and was treated as a mini-paragraph – a guide to the reader to take a new breath. Systems of punctuation have differed greatly in the degree to which they have attempted to guide *performance*, and Jerome's enthusiasm for this cause was later echoed by Charlemagne's. In the meantime, but particularly during the seventh and eighth centuries, other significant changes were taking place. Chief among them was the emergence of lower-case handwriting, with its consequent loss of evenness of letter height, while in England,

Ireland and Germany scribes to whom Latin was increasingly an alien as well as a foreign language began to write it out in separated words. A final space became conventional in dividing sentences, with an enlarged letter at the start of both sentences and paragraphs.

One manuscript of the *Anglo-Saxon Chronicle* uses only two symbols. The more frequent is: $\vee$, occurring at the end of each yearly entry, which may be one sentence long or comprise many 'sentences' over several pages. Within entries there are twelve instances of some kind of pointing, using either this mark or something like a semi-colon; evidently some lesser break is intended, but there is no obvious syntactic point in the placing of either mark.[3]

It was an Englishman working at Charlemagne's court who developed and promoted, as part of a range of educational reforms, the basis of our current punctuation system. Alcuin of York co-operated with his master on a new style of script, on the regularisation of spelling and, as a logical adjunct to those, a way of marking biblical and liturgical manuscripts. The first signs of the new system are evident in the earliest instances of the new Carolingian minuscule script produced at Corbie and Aachen in the last two decades of the eighth century. With the influence of empire it spread rapidly through Europe, and by the twelfth century was virtually universal and standard. Its main revolutionary features were the establishment of standardised marks and the introduction of some new ones. The point (or *punctus*) was still used to mark off phrases, and a group of points to show the ends of sentences. The signs (*neums*) used in the musical notation of Gregorian plainchant to indicate a pattern of rising or falling intonation were the *punctus elevatus* (✓) and the *punctus interrogativus*, of much the same shape as the modern question mark but tilted to the right.

The boldness of this has hardly been matched since. Although (as we shall see shortly) systems of punctuation have been used to facilitate reading, there has not been since Alcuin any substantial effort to develop a notation for *performance* analogous to that for singers, who are guided in terms of pitch, tempo, volume, and so on. The Carolingian system, then, indicated not only pauses necessitated by syntactic structure but also vocal inflections. This impulse was continued and sophisticated in the twelfth century by the addition of the *punctus circumflexus* (⸖); its purpose was to indicate a rising inflection at the end of a subordinate clause, especially when the grammatical sense of the sentence was still incomplete. Later systems highlight either syntactical structure or vocal convenience; only this attempted to accommodate both intentions and, in addition, guided interpretative performance. The system continued to evolve between the tenth and thirteenth centuries, particularly under the attention paid to liturgical manuscripts; monastic orders especially had a vested interest in an inflectional system that facilitated effective reading aloud in chapel, cloister and refectory. Here are the origins of the *colon* still used to divide verses of the Psalms in breviaries and prayer books. The hyphen, used to indicate the continuity of words broken at the end of lines, appeared, single, late in the tenth century, and was often doubled between the fourteenth and eighteenth centuries.

The later Middle Ages saw the introduction of more, helpful, signs, but the use of the system became generally more careless, particularly in secular hands. In thirteenth- and fourteenth-century university texts (at Paris, Bologna and Oxford) a sort of paragraph mark based on *c* for *capitulum* ('little head(ing)' or 'chapter') is frequent at the start of sentences. The virgule (/) becomes an extra form of light stop. This is the period of the first printed texts of the Bible, and these, prepared by clerical scribes, carefully observe the inflectional rules. The early English texts of Caxton, by contrast, are a mess of points and virgules that pays little attention to syntax. Parentheses, used much as now, have appeared by about 1500. Yet, notwithstanding the increasing repertoire of marks available to them, lawyers were producing documents entirely without punctuation; this practice persists in the tendency of modern-day lawyers to punctuate only very lightly, though whether in the hope of eliminating ambiguity or of fostering it is not – now as then – clear.

The finalisation of what is recognisably our

modern system owes much to the Venetian printer 'Aldus Manutius' (Aldo Manuzio, died 1515). Recognising the permanency of books as artefacts, and – sharp businessman that he was – that rich people would buy them for private use, he began to tidy up the humanistic system refined by Italian scribes of the previous century as they copied classical and contemporary Latin texts. Until around 1450 the simple point and *punctus elevatus* were preferred for the minor pauses, and thereafter were replaced by the virgule and what is now called the colon (:). The virgule, originally placed towards the top of letters, was brought down to the line, where, to avoid becoming entangled with letters on the line below, it developed a curve – that is, it became a comma (modern French *virgule*). Manutius tidied all this up, but, seeing a change in the market from texts to be read aloud to texts for silent reading, he modified the medieval, rhetoric-based system to a grammar-based one. His grandson of the same name formulated it in *Orthographiae Ratio* (1566), which included (to give them the names by which they were known in seventeenth-century England) the period or full stop, colon, semi-colon and comma; by 1660 these had been joined by the exclamation mark, quotation marks and the dash.

Differences between the English system and those in the rest of Europe are few and slight, given their common origins in the work of the Italian and French printers of the fifteenth and sixteenth centuries. We may briefly note: French introduces quotations with a dash, sometimes marking them with guillemets (« »); from the eighteenth century Spanish has used inverted question and exclamation marks at the beginning of questions and exclamations as well as the normal ones (thus *¿Donde?* – 'Where?'), with quotations marked in either the French or the English way; German, working on rules propounded in 1781, uses a severely syntactical system, all relative clauses and all clauses introduced by *dass* ('that') being preceded by a comma; quotations are marked either by pairs of commas on a downstairs–upstairs principle („ ") or by reversed guillemets (» «). For emphasis, German uses letter-spacing as well as italic type. The earliest Russian punctuation was based on Greek models, since the Cyrillic alphabet is derived from the Greek. From the eighteenth century Russian has used the systems evident elsewhere in Europe but with a syntactic emphasis even heavier than that used in Germany, in particular an even wider obligatory use of commas with subordinate and some co-ordinate clauses.

To conclude this section, it is appropriate to say something of punctuation in Shakespeare, particularly as he was writing at a time when the system was at an interesting stage of development.[4] The situation as regards his own practice is complicated by the fact that we have very little in Shakespeare's hand and no original manuscripts of the works in the First Folio, and by the different habits and preferences of the various compositors who prepared his work for the press. It may be, of course, that these all reproduce faithfully Shakespeare's own wildly inconsistent practice, but this is improbable. By 1600, as we have seen, pauses (whether dramatic or grammatical) could be marked by full stop, colon, semi-colon or comma. The comma (replacing the virgule from 1530 or so) and the semi-colon were introduced in the sixteenth century; the semi-colon is first recorded in the 1530s but did not enter regular use until later in the century. The development from marks used to indicate pauses in texts read aloud to an illiterate (or literate) medieval audience to marks indicating grammatical structure for a literate readership is not as clear-cut as it might be, since pause and structure will often coincide, not least in dramatic texts. There is evidence from the early seventeenth century that if a writer's manuscript was punctuated lightly a compositor would feel at liberty to include additional marks: as a rule of thumb, the later the edition of a text in this period, the heavier the punctuation. So, as regards Shakespeare, the Folio text of 1623 may be assumed to be much further from his punctuation mannerisms than are the quarto volumes of the 1590s. Again, habits differ among the compositors; one of those who worked on the Folio was particularly given to semi-colons, while two who worked on the Sonnets dealt differently with the ends of quatrains. As his recent editors say, therefore, 'we can . . . draw few specific interpretive conclusions about Shake-speare's practice from the punctuation which we find in the printed text'.[5]

The question mark and the exclamation mark (called in *The Winter's Tale* the 'note of admiration') are used almost indiscriminately, each frequently appearing where modern usage would expect the other. The 'apostraphus', as it is called in *Love's Labour's Lost*, was much used for elision. If we trust the evidence of the verse, then *crooked*, for example, could be pronounced (and written) either as *crooked* or as *crook'd*; similarly *aged* and *learned* could be *ag'd* and *learn'd*. Examples of Shakespearean elision include forms such as *look'd*, *mark'd* and manage-ment of the third-person present singular in forms such as *liu'st*. We have now lost this choice of pronunciations, but Shakespeare could indicate his metrical preference on any one occasion either by spelling (*talkt*) or by apostrophe (*talk'd*). In the work of compositor Crane genitive *'s* is found: *odd's*, *it's* (not *its*); it is used also with names ending in a vowel. Elsewhere the apostrophe is used without consistency or apparent purpose (*applau'd*, *dos't*, *go'st*, *endu'rd*). One group to whom such usages might have made sense were the printers. These would often use ligatures (ct, fi, fl, ff etc.) – single pieces of type holding two letters often found in combination: hence, probably, *accur'st* and *expre'st*, *st* being printed together in a single piece (as ſt), and the apostrophe being thereby forced to precede rather than follow the long *s*.

Crane also makes much use of parenthesis, particularly for vocatives and exclamations – e.g. *what (the hell)*; he was fond also of single hyphens in what he mistakenly took to be compound words: *viza-ments, put-off*. The editions prepared closest in time to Shakespeare's manuscripts indicate that Shakespeare himself made much less, indeed little, use of parentheses, hyphens and apostrophes.

Three further conventions (or habits) of Elizabethan punctuation are worth mentioning as very different from modern practice. First, brackets were sometimes used to do the work of commas and dashes, and thus are often opened without being closed, and vice versa. Secondly, to highlight proverbs, maxims and other *sententiae*, double inverted commas would be placed at the start, but with no 'closing' pair at the end; this device was sometimes coupled with the use of italics. At the same time, there is use of the comma where we would expect a hyphen (and where Shakespeare evidently intended a compound): so, we find *active, valiant* where we would now expect *active-valiant*. There are signs, though, that Shakespeare thought of the comma *as* a hyphen: in *Hamlet* he writes that peace should 'stand a comma 'tween their amities', where 'comma' seems to mean a link or connection.

Lastly, there is a distinctive use of italics and capitals. In manuscript different forms could be used to give emphasis – in particular, manuscripts mainly in the Elizabethan 'secretary' hand highlight items with the more legible italic recently introduced from Italy. Shakespeare's printers used italic for personal names, place-names and quotations from other languages; to indicate something an actor needed to stress; and to mark off items such as letters and songs from mainstream dialogue. Occasionally, as with *interim* in *Henry V*, italic would be used for an unusual word, such as a recent borrowing from Latin. Printed texts continued the manuscript tradition of marking paragraphs, sentences and proper nouns with capitals; though different printers had different styles, it is evident, especially from the Folio, that Shakespeare's printers were moving towards the capitalisation of all nouns.

SYSTEMS

With the vast majority of the marks effectively in place by 1600, the history of punctuation in England since then is largely a matter of divided attitudes to how they should be used. Before then, the punctuation of English texts had been as unsystematic as that of texts in other languages; and when Caxton started printing he found this as much a muddle as other aspects of the written language, particularly in poetic texts, which frequently had no punctuation at all. In *Beowulf* the only punctuation mark was the full stop, and this was true also of Chaucer's manuscripts, where it appeared only at the end of lines, regardless of whether or not a sentence ended there. Other Chaucerian manuscripts had the virgule (or virgil or oblique: /) at the middle of lines. Wyclif's manuscripts were more heavily punctuated but in a way that looks to us odd:

> forsoþe if ȝee shulen forȝeue to men her synnys : & oure heuenly fadir . shal forȝeue to ȝou ȝoure trespassis / so 'þely [the less] if ȝee shulen forȝeue not to men : neiþ [neither] oure fadir shal forȝeue to ȝou ȝoure synnes. But . . . .[6]

This second sentence begins with a capital letter, but the first does not. The long first sentence is divided at the middle by a virgule, and each half is subdivided by a colon, but the system underlying this is as unclear as the reason for the full stop after the first colon.

Caxton was a kind of man-in-the-middle between the system in which punctuation was determined and dominated by considerations of elocution and that determined by syntax, and consequently his own punctuation shows no discernible rationale. One might, for instance, think of his virgule as equivalent to a modern comma, but in 'vyrgyle / ouyde . tullye . [Virgil, Ovid, Tully] and all the other noble poetes' he uses both the virgule and the full stop for that purpose. In some places, indeed, the virgule seems more like a full stop and vice versa:

And whan I had aduysed me in this sayd boke.
I delybered and concluded to translate it in to
englysshe   And forthwyth toke a penne & ynke
and wrote a leef or tweyne / whyche I ouersawe
agayn to correcte it.

Chapter 6 will bear out the judgement of the
commentator who found Caxton used his marks
'arbitrarily as to power'.[7] The same is true of his
successor, Wynkyn de Worde. Tyndale's Bible
(1526) still followed the older style of prose
punctuation:

For ād [and] yff yeshall forgeve other men there
trespases / youre father ī hevē [in heaven] shal
also forgeve you. but ād ye wyll not forgeve men
there trespases. Moreovre . . . .

The elocutionary system

The earliest systems of punctuation, then, both
reflected the way words are spoken, and eventually
began to guide the reader towards a spoken performance of a written text. It may be that Greek
scribes ran words together at least partly because
that is what we tend to do in speaking; there are
no more pauses in *kiss of death* than in *punctuation*.
Exclamation and question marks acknowledge the
difference in tone that normally goes with such
utterances. Yet such a system relies essentially

upon a fallacy, upon a failure to recognise that writing and speech are two wholly separate forms of discourse, as different as ballet from blank verse. I make an exception here of the early monastic intention to mark a text for reading aloud; that is a case in which the written text has only the same relation to the purpose as has a musical score to a performance. But – to push this to its conclusion – any elocutionary system that intended to mark all written texts as if for vocal performance would quickly run into problems impossible to solve. To begin with, for a system to represent even non-rhetorical, everyday speech there would be needed an enormously elaborate system of signs to cope with the variations of pitch, tone, pace, volume and other factors. Given that some people cannot even manage the simple apostrophe, there seems little prospect of joy in such an undertaking. An unhelpful legacy of this attitude is the nonsense that different stops represent different lengths of pause (see end of Chapter 2).

The grammatical principle

If Caxton was confused, his successors soon brought English under a system of controls that seem familiar to us. Caxton died in 1491, and by the publication of Holinshed's *Chronicles* (1587), a frequent read of Shakespeare's, William Harrison was writing this about the language:

> But as this excellencie of the English toong is
> found in one, and the south part of this Iland;
> so in Wales the greatest number (as I said) retaine
> still their owne ancient language, that of the
> north part of the said countrie being lesse corrup-
> ted than the other, and therefore reputed for the
> better in their owne estimation and judgement.[8]

The spelling here has a familiar look about it, but
what makes the passage really accessible is the
punctuation: a syntactically balanced sentence ('as
. . . so . . . ') is divided by a semi-colon, regardless
of the length of the sentence overall, and the semi-
colon is not at a convenient breathing-point; the
aside 'as I said' is appropriately within parentheses,
and commas are used throughout in relation to
clauses and participial phrases.

Ben Jonson (1572–1637) was an early advocate
of syntactical punctuation. Though he was still
capable, with a dramatist's ear, of making connec-
tions between stops and pauses (for 'our breath is
by nature so short'),[4] his practice is that of one
of the very few early dramatists who carefully
controlled the printed versions of their work.

The insistence on using punctuation to show the
grammatical construction of a piece reached its
fullest development in the eighteenth century and,
albeit slightly modified, dominated the training
received by people who were at school before
the mid-1960s. Here is an example of eighteenth-
century practice:

While that great body was invaded by open violence, or undermined by slow decay, a pure and humble religion gently insinuated itself into the minds of men, grew up in silence and obscurity, derived new vigour from opposition, and finally erected the triumphant banner of the cross on the ruins of the Capitol.

> Edward Gibbon, *The Decline and Fall of the Roman Empire* (1776–88) ch. 15

And another:

In this work, when it shall be found that much is omitted, let it not be forgotten that much likewise is performed; and though no book was ever spared out of tenderness to the author, and the world is little solicitous to know whence proceeded the faults of that which it condemns; yet it may gratify curiosity to inform it, that the *English Dictionary* was written with little assistance of the learned, and without any patronage of the great; not in the soft obscurities of retirement, or under the shelter of academick bowers, but amidst inconvenience and distraction, in sickness and in sorrow.

> Samuel Johnson, *Preface to a Dictionary of the English Language* (1755)

That this is in any case writing of the highest order only makes it easier to see how the punctuation works and helps heighten the rhetorical effectiveness of these passages. In one respect only, apart from its greatness, does this differ from most educated practice today. Modern punctuation has dropped the comma before noun clauses in sentences such as 'He declared, that he was for it'. Two passages from Sir Walter Scott will allow us to identify some other changes from eighteenth- and nineteenth-century usage:

> 'The storm,' said the stranger, 'must be an apology for waiving ceremony – his daughter's health was weak – she had suffered much from a recent alarm – he trusted their intrusion on the Master of Ravenswood's hospitality would not be altogether unpardonable in the circumstances of the case – his child's safety must be dearer to him than ceremony.'
>
> *The Bride of Lammermoor* (1819) ch. 9

> I replied, 'that he confounded the operations of the pencil and the pen . . . .'
>
> Ibid., ch. 1

> 'Sir, (said he) you are for making a monarchy of what should be a republick.'
>
> Boswell, *Life of Johnson* (1791), 1773

What we chiefly notice here is the inclusion of 'said he' within parentheses, and other changes concern the use of inverted commas for indirect speech. Now we would exclude the *that* as not being among the words actually spoken. But the major point of difference is the liberality with which punctuation marks are used. A passage of Boswell:

> This was experienced by Johnson, when he became the fervent admirer of Mrs. Porter, after her first husband's death. Miss Porter told me, that when he was first introduced to her mother, his appearance was very forbidding . . . .
>
> James Boswell, *Life of Johnson* (1791), 1734

To the final row of omission dots this has six punctuation marks, whereas modern practice would probably have only the obligatory two – the apostrophe in *husband's* and the full stop after *death*; modern practice, that is, would have none of the extras used by Boswell. Such 'overstopping' in modern texts would be acceptable only where there was a high degree of technicality and such elaborateness of punctuation was required to eliminate ambiguity. In ordinary contexts there is no justification for this kind of thing, however 'correct':

> Jeannie, too, is, just occasionally, like a good girl out of a book.

> Shakespeare, it is true, had, as I have said, as respects England, the privilege which only first-comers enjoy.[9]

Such practice serves no good purpose: it is not required by any complexity of sentence structure, and reflects no intelligible style of vocal delivery. There are some hard cases, particularly in literary contexts. Conrad's *Heart of Darkness* and *Lord Jim*, in both of which a narrator recounts conversations, have this sort of thing, which can seem bewildering:

> ' " 'Ah! it's you. Lend a hand quick.'
>
> ' "That's what he said. Quick! As if anybody could be quick enough. 'Aren't you going to do something?' I asked.
>
> ' " 'Yes. Clear out,' he snarled over his shoulder.
>
> Joseph Conrad, *Lord Jim* (1900) ch. 8

Where you have a narrator recounting what other people have said, as well as reporting his own part in conversations (Ford's *The Good Soldier* is another example), virtually every paragraph begins with one or more sets of inverted commas.

The minimalist principle

The Fowlers were the first to set about the elimination of overstopping: 'the objection to full stopping that is correct is the discomfort inflicted on readers, who are perpetually being checked like a horse with a fidgety driver'.[10] The same point is made with unconscious hilarity by the author of the *Chambers' Encyclopaedia* (1923) article on 'Punctuation': 'Use commas and semicolons sparingly, especially commas; use them, indeed, only where they are absolutely necessary'. Modern practice follows this precept, if not this example.

Where overstopping does occur, it is usually a matter of too generous a use of the comma, and more will be said about that in the relevant section. In the meantime readers can consider their punctuation behaviour in relation to the use of a comma after adverbs or adverb phrases in sentences such as 'In August, the results will be published'. No comma is needed here, any more than in 'the results will be published, in August'. Common expressions that attract otiose commas are *perhaps* and *probably*, *indeed*, *certainly* and *apparently*, *on the whole*, *by and large*, *in the main*, and (when used as conjunctives) *now*, *then*, *for*, *because*, *yet* and *nevertheless*.

Understopping nevertheless carries with it the risk of confusion if pursued to minimalist extremes. The generally creditable desire to avoid excess, and the less self-evidently creditable concern for the look of a page that preoccupies many publishers, can neglect the reader and the reader's convenience. Naturally there must be adequate punctuation where there is the possibility of ambiguity or temporary puzzlement. Consider the importance of the comma in

After all, his work was not wasted.

Further, on looking more closely he spotted a clue.

In 1984, 200 more students were admitted.

Writers today (or their editors) are much committed to this lighter style of punctuation, not always with happy results:

> From here
> he will see what appears to be a town in the heat
> distorted distance.
>
> J. G. Farrell,
> *The Siege of Krishnapur* (1973) ch. 1

A hyphen here would have been a help, and although the modern practice has much to recommend it one can still learn a lot about a writer and a writer's concern for the reader by noting how (in particular) hyphens and commas are used. Writer and printer and editor would do well to recognise that all their endeavours are ultimately for the reader and the reader's delight, instruction, understanding, and so on. In the light of this we can now identify three principles that should govern the best practice in punctuation today.

Principles

1   **Use as much as you need.**

2   **Use as little as you need.**

3   **And the greatest of these is clarity.**

LITERARY POINTS

Something of the crucial role of punctuation in complex literary texts may be seen in three instances from the work of Dr Johnson, Keats and Henry James.

1   Keats's 'Ode on a Grecian Urn' is a notoriously difficult poem, the complexities of its line of argument further complicated by uncertainty as to how it should be punctuated. The situation is not helped by the fact that the two major cruces are right at the beginning and right at the end.

In its familiar form the first line runs,

Thou still unravish'd bride of quietness . . . .

As one of the best commentators on Keats points out, 'the essence of the urn is its potentiality waiting to be fulfilled'.[11] With this in mind we may regard the poem's opening line as offering an image of continuing virginity – 'still unravished' being the equivalent of 'yet to be ravished'. But as first printed the line looks like this:

Thou still, unravish'd bride of quietness . . . .[12]

The adverbial *still* of the first version now becomes an adjective, and the meaning of the line is now re-routed to give the sense of a bride lying still in expectancy. It matters little that Keats's intentions in this line are probably now irrecoverable, since the two possibilities play nicely together and are not in conflict.

Much more problematic are the last two lines. Again as Bate puts the matter, the 'perennially disputed close of the poem has generated discussion . . . which already fills a small book of critical essays'.[13] The problem might be formulated briefly as: who is saying what to whom?

Standard editions of Keats's poems print the lines as they appeared in his 1820 volume, which, as Bate reminds us, Keats 'was probably too ill to oversee':[14]

'Beauty is truth, truth beauty,' – that is all
Ye know on earth, and all ye need to know.

On this reading the last line and a half is the poet's own judgement on the preceding, more or less meaningless, aphorism, intended either as consolation to his readers ('Ye' – though he has previously been speaking of mankind as 'us') or as an obeisance to the figures depicted on the urn (though the general thrust of this final stanza is what the urn, as a 'friend', can offer to mankind). The first published appearance of the lines, however (in *Annals of the Fine Arts*), was:

Beauty is truth, truth beauty. – That is all
Ye know on earth, and all ye need to know.

Taken together, the two readings offer three possibilities: either both lines are spoken by the urn to the reader but the particular sententiousness of the first five words call for special pointing; or the first five words are spoken by the urn to the reader and the following words by the poet to the reader; or the first five words are spoken by the urn and the remainder by the poet to the figures depicted on it (surely the least persuasive of the possible readings). Given that Keats was unable to oversee publication, recourse may be had to manuscripts (none of them, sadly, a holograph), but here there is no help. Four contemporary transcripts exist:

(a)   Beauty is truth, – Truth Beauty, – that is all
       Ye know on earth, and all ye need to know.

(b)   Beauty is truth, – truth beauty, – that is all
       Ye know on earth, and all ye need to know.

(c)   Beauty is Truth, – Truth Beauty, – that is all
       Ye know on earth, and all ye need to know.

(d)   Beauty is Truth, – Truth beauty, – That is all
       Ye know on earth, and all ye need to know.[15]

So all four transcripts dispense with the inverted commas and the full stop of the *Annals* and the 1820 volume respectively, and introduce additional dashes and different patterns of capitalisation. Where the poem's meaning really lies is ultimately a matter for the literary critic to determine, but it is not a decision that can be made without attending to the definitive punctuation, whichever it may be.

2   The case with Dr Johnson is rather a matter of convention than one of meaning. Donald Greene, editor of a selection of Johnson's work for the Oxford Authors series, tells of receiving an irate letter from one of his readers.[16] The correspondent's complaint concerned the editor's punctuation of Johnson's famous letter to Lord Chesterfield (reproduced on pp. 182–4 of this book), in particular the sentence about the belated 'notice' Chesterfield had taken of Johnson's labours on the *Dictionary*: 'It has been delayed till I am indifferent and cannot enjoy it, till I am solitary and cannot impart it, till I am known and do not want it'. The complainant's point was that (as everyone knows) the commas separating these subordinate clauses should be semi-colons.

Greene's response easily disposes of the complaint as a matter of fact, and raises interesting, wider issues about the conventions of punctuating printed texts in the eighteenth century. As for the letter in particular, Greene followed the standard text as given in R. W. Chapman's edition of Johnson's letters. There Chapman points out that the original of the letter is long lost and that he therefore used the text as later dictated by Johnson to Baretti, which Johnson then re-read. The manuscript of this version is in the British Library, and it is from this version that Boswell made the copy he used in the *Life*. The copy Boswell sent to his printer (which is now at Yale) has no punctuation at all between the clauses. It follows, therefore, that the semi-colons so lamented of Greene's correspondent were the work of the printers of Boswell's *Life*; and they, as Chapman points out, 'grossly over-pointed the letters'; 'Johnson's punctuation,' Chapman goes on, 'though it is not always careful, is far better suited to his current style than is the heavier punctuation of the eighteenth- and nineteenth-century editors'.[17]

It is not a large step from the details of this case to the general perception of the eighteenth century as a period in which writers pointed their texts very heavily. Greene quotes an instance of this prejudice:

> What was the satisfactory modernized system of pointing for Dr. Johnson, with its heavy syntactical notation . . . is not a satisfactory guide for the present-day reader [of Shakespearean texts] . . . Shakespeare did not write in logically pointed Johnsonian periods.[18]

Whatever may be the truth of the matter as regards Elizabethan texts, it is harsh to make Johnson carry the can for the practice of the printers of his day. Far from there being evidence that their 'heavy syntactical punctuation' was 'satisfactory' for him, the signs we have point the other way. The light punctuation of the manuscripts we have suggests that Johnson's preferences differed from those of his printers. Yet the image of heavy punctuation remains. The Yale editors of the *Rambler* draw attention to 'Johnson's ready acquiescence in [printing-] house styles' of spelling and punctuation, in editions of his works, something he had in common with (one presumes) many other writers of his day, who had not the indulgence of the *laisser passer* attitude that leads current editors and publishers to accept, by and large, what authors submit to them.[19]

Johnson is caught in a trap here. We know that Johnson loved logical and periodic syntax, so he must somehow be responsible for the 'heavy syntactical' punctuation of his published writings. How do we know this? Why, from the way his printed works are punctuated. Greene properly suggests that it might be instructive to examine the preferences evident in Johnson's manuscripts in the light of a study of the house styles of, say, the *Gentleman's Magazine*.

3 According to how you think of Henry James and his working methods, you will call up the word 'meticulous' or the word 'finicking'. Perhaps the present ambiguity of 'fastidious' could satisfy both parties. Whatever judgement readers make of the results, James certainly worked and re-worked his texts with an assiduity almost unmatched by that of any other major figure. A recent study

highlights the degree to which an attention to punctuation featured in these re-workings.[20]

The point is convincingly made that a comparison of successive drafts and versions of *The Turn of the Screw* 'leads us to understand things about the text of the story that we would otherwise not be able to see so easily'. What is revealed by a study of this famously controversial text is 'an author intent on establishing a text that cannot be interpreted in a definite way'. A key document in being alert to the importance of punctuation to James is a letter he wrote to his agent about a proposal from the English publisher Martin Secker for a new edition of the tale; James agreed on the 'distinct understanding, please, that he conform *literatim* and punctuation to [the New York edition] text – to the last comma or rather, more essentially, no-comma'.[21] An insistence that existing punctuation be honoured is easily understood. More puzzling at first glance is the last stipulation, particularly with its nonce-hyphenation, *no-comma*, which unavoidably suggests something stronger than 'no commas' would have done. Paradoxically the negative assumes a positive force, such that it is not a matter of cutting down on the commas for something like the reader's convenience or the appearance of the printed page but of an insistence that their use would import unwanted semantic effects. (It has been suggested that, once he had become used to dictating his work, eschewing commas, James returned to earlier texts – *The Turn*

of the Screw was first published in 1898 – to bring
them into line with his later practice. This does not
meet the facts, since it can be shown that in his
1908 revision James not only deletes some commas
but also adds some.[22]) There is insufficient room
here to detail the alterations he makes to the
punctuation of his tale. A single instance must
serve, with an exhortation to return to the original
with an eye on the fact that all James's changes have
as their purpose to make the story as ambiguous as
lexical and punctuational changes can manage.

Consider this sentence from near the end of
chapter 9:

> I can say now neither what determined nor what
> guided me, but I went straight along the lobby,
> holding my candle high, till I came within sight
> of the tall window that presided over the great
> turn of the staircase.

There are difficulties with the first part of this
sentence, as far as the *but*, in terms both of itself
and of its relationship with what follows: first, this
introductory material seems to make a statement
about the narrator's present state of mind (*I can
say now* . . .), whereas what follows the *but* is a
statement about a subsequent state of mind, that
may or may not have been influenced by later
knowledge; secondly, the *but* may therefore be a
way of contrasting two periods of time (then and
after/now), or, thirdly, it may have the effect of

'but to go on with my story'. These are not of course matters of punctuation, but they do establish a field of semantic uncertainty which is developed in the second part of the sentence where punctuation does establish the same effect.

The clauses following the *but* may be read with the following sentences as a model:

(a)   John walked along the road until he came to a pub.

(b)   John walked along the road, until he came to a pub.

(c)   John walked along the road, with a map in his hand, until he came to a pub.

One difference between (a) and (b) is clearly that (a) suggests purpose, whereas in (b) the coming to a pub is merely accidental, a contingent part of the walk. A further difference is that in (a) we are given the consciousness of John, whereas in (b) it is the narrator's observation. With the intervention of a middle clause in (c), the earlier distinctions are lost – or, rather, blurred. The middle adverbial clause (which could have gone elsewhere, in front of *John*) is marked off with commas, as it has to be here; but it is not clear whether these commas are also separating the clauses as we had them in (a) and (b). Applying these lessons to the sentence from Henry James (. . . *I went straight along the lobby, holding my candle high, till I came within sight of the tall window* . . .), we see that the intervention of the clause *holding my candle high* ambiguates the relationship between *lobby* and *till*. Was there purpose there or not?

The character's purpose may be problematic, but a consideration of James's revisions as a whole concerning his use of commas reveals unanswerably that he at any rate was quite clear what he was doing.

2

All the Stops and Pretty Whiles

---

*Full stop (period) – colon – semi-colon – comma –
question mark – exclamation mark*

FULL STOP

> *Where I have come, great clerks have purposed*
> *To greet me with premeditated welcomes;*
> *Where I have seen them shiver and look pale,*
> *Make periods in the midst of sentences . . . .*
> Shakespeare, *A Midsummer Night's*
> *Dream*, v.i.91–4

The full stop, or full point, is more commonly
referred to in America as the period.

Time was when every schoolboy knew that a full
stop came at the end of a sentence and was followed

40

by a space and a capital letter.* Time is, however, that not only schoolboys and schoolgirls but also tabloid journalists and advanced novelists seem not to know this. It is hard to be sure if this is more frequently from ignorance or from modish affectation. It is outside the scope of this little book to correct any ignorance of what constitutes a sentence, but a work on punctuation, however small, cannot fail to condemn both the spraying of a text with commas where there should be full stops and the use of full stops to mark off what are only subordinate clauses. A commonly allowable exception is that which occurs when, *for good reason*, an independent thought may be marked off separately even if it is not technically a sentence; this is particularly so when a comment is made that

---

* Until recently one would have thought it a waste of space to point out that a capital letter is used not only at the start of a sentence but also at the beginning of titles and names. But this simple convention is under threat from graphic designers, its position highlighted in a recent television-review: 'Of all the non-human deaths reported this century – most famously God and Socialism – one has received too little attention. Someone is killing the capital letter. Last night's *Signals* (C4) was presented, according to the captions, by morwenna banks, who would once have been plain Morwenna Banks, and was introducing a film called *the day comics grew up*. An hour later, the strange case of the lower case was thickening. *Signals* does not yet have the courage to be *signals* but *thirtysomething* (C4), the programme which follows it, has no time for being *Thirtysomething* or indeed, having murdered the hyphen and the word space as well, *Thirty Something*' (Mark Lawson, *Independent*, 19 January 1989, p. 14).

effectively suggests a tone or attitude to something said immediately before: 'She said she would kill herself if I left her. A likely story'. Exceptions are always available to genius. The opening of Dickens' *Bleak House* (1852–3) is a sequence of 'sentences' which, however 'irregular', could make their rhetorical effect with no other system of marks:

> London. Michaelmas term lately over, and the Lord Chancellor sitting in Lincoln's Hall. Implacable November weather. As much mud in the streets, as if the waters had but newly retired from the face of the earth, and it would not be wonderful to meet a Megalosaurus, forty feet long or so, waddling like an elephantine lizard up Holborn Hill.

How different from two sadly typical pieces of contemporary fashion-mongering – the first from journalism, the second from fiction:

> There is an earthiness about Eartha Kitt. The earthiness of a woman who will suddenly lean across the table as you sit with her, gather up your salad in her hands, and transfer it, without explanation, to her plate. The earthiness of a woman who lets you know when she has tired of you . . . .
>
> *Sunday Times Magazine*, July 1988

Oh, boy. What a week.

Fourteen muggings, three rapes, a knifing on Culver Avenue, thirty-six assorted burglaries, and the squadroom being painted.

Not that the squadroom didn't *need* painting.

Ed McBain, Fuzz (1968) ch. 1

Oh, boy.

Three paragraphs and not a single sentence.

And it's no defence to say that it's a *genre* novel.

Before considering other uses of the full stop, let us note that (a) when a sentence ends with a question mark or exclamation mark, these supersede the full stop, and (b) the place of a full stop in relation to inverted commas will be discussed under that heading.

The other major use of the full stop is with abbreviations, which may be regarded under a number of headings.

Short forms

Previous discussion has involved distinctions between contractions, where the last letter of the abbreviation is also the last letter of the full word (e.g. *Mr, Fr, Sgt*) and abbreviations properly so called (e.g. *MS, RSVP*). In *Modern English Usage* Fowler proposed, partly as a counter to overstopping, that no stop be used after contractions. This is well intentioned and generally workable but meets problems when plurals are formed with *s* (*mac, prefab*). All in all, particularly under the influence of the minimalist principle and the tendency of many shortened forms to become effectively words in their own right, it is now much commoner and simpler for full stops not to be used. So:

1 No stop for *Mr, Mrs, Dr, Fr, Sgt, Cpl*, and so on, but it would be well to distinguish between a *Coy. Commander* and a *Coy Commander*. (*Ms*, it seems, wishes to be thought of as neither an abbreviation nor a contraction; if it survives at all it will probably do so without a stop.)

2 Items such as *pram, taxi* and *exam* may now be regarded as independent words needing no stop.

3 Similarly names that are now familiar in shortened forms (*Tom, Will*) need no stop but *Chas., Geo.* and *Wm.* do.

4 For reasons of history rather than logic, old county names when abbreviated take a stop, with the exception of *Hants, Northants* and *Salop*; this no longer seems a sensible distinction. (What you do with abominations such as *Gtr Manchester* is ignore them until they go away.)

5 No stop is used in giving the genitive of an

abbreviation; thus *J. & J. Sutcliffe and Co.* but *J. & J. Sutcliffe and Co's tripe products*.

6 Note these uses with small initials: *a.m.; p.m.; i.e.; cf.; pp.* (In this last example *p.p.* would be wrong, as the initial is duplicated to indicate a plural.)

Initials

The traditional rule has been to use a full stop after every letter that represents a word (P.T.O., R.S.V.P.), but with combinations a stop is used only after the last letter, because the first does not represent a separate word (*MS.* and its modern offspring TS. [typescript]; *TV.*). What was a tendency has now become a fixed practice: where series of initials are particularly familiar, or easily spoken or form an acronym, stops may be dispensed with (*BBC, NATO, AIDS, STD, PAYE*).

Latin words

The decline in the teaching of the classical languages puts at risk of error the hardy writer who attempts a Latin phrase without knowing if its common English form is an abbreviation or not. Most frequently got wrong are (doubly abbreviated) *nem. con., verb. sap.*; (part-abbreviated) *ad lib., infra dig.*; (not abbreviated) *pro rata, sine die. Re* is not an abbreviation.

Odds and sods

1   For points of the compass use one stop, if any (*NW., SE.*), but for London postal districts use two (*N.W.6, S.E.1*) unless you are using the postcode, in which case use none at all.

2   Short forms that mix upper- and lower-case letters require full points (*I.o.W., Esq., Ph.D., B.Mus.*); exceptions are *Mr, Mrs, Mme, Mlle, St* (Saint); days and months are conventionally marked as follows:

Sun. Mon. Tue. Wed. Thurs. Fri. Sat.
Jan. Feb. Mar. Apr. May June
July Aug. Sept. Oct. Nov. Dec.

(I have seen *June* given as *Jun.*, but you'd really have to be in a hurry to need that.)

3   *4to* and *8mo*, like *1st* and *2nd*, are symbols, not abbreviations, and take no points; *lb., oz.*, if anyone still uses them, are right for both singular and plural; metric measures are generally printed without points in their short forms (*cm, kg*).

4   *OED* and *COD* and *DNB* (*Oxford English Diction-*

ary, *Concise Oxford Dictionary*, *Dictionary of National Biography*), etc.; *Saint* is generally *St* but may be *S.* (in both cases, plural *SS.*) – French saints have *St-* for men and *Ste-* for women: *H-bomb*, *ITV*, *C* (Celsius or centigrade) and *F* (Fahrenheit).

Lastly it is worth noting that the full stop, or period, has lately become fashionable as something spoken as well as written:

> All the pieces collected in this book were prompted by invitation or impulse to 'write on' something or other. . . . They also witness to a compulsion, which virtually defines the professional writer, to write on, period.
>
> David Lodge, Foreword to *Write On* (1986)

COLON

> *The Bible bars the dash, which is the great refuge of those who are too lazy to punctuate. I never use it when I can possibly substitute the colon, and I save up the colon jealously for certain effects which no other stop produces. As you have no rules, and sometimes throw colons about with an unhinged mind, here are some rough rules for you.*
>
> G. B. Shaw, letter to T. E. Lawrence,
> 7 October 1924

The colon is not often used nowadays. As we have seen, its earliest use was as a marker in biblical texts. Its season of fullest flower was the eighteenth century, when elaborate sentence structures (properly called periodic) were much more common than they are today, when, even in literary contexts, the tendency is to a sort of staccato brevity. Despite the view expressed in 1829 that the colon and semi-colon are 'primeval sources of improfitable contention', it would be pleasing to see some revival of life in the colon; yet one may add, at the risk of sounding inconsistent, that at its best it is an instrument of some subtlety, and therefore best used sparingly. Its simplest technical functions are quickly indicated.

1 It offers detailed elaboration of a preceding statement:

> The past is a foreign country: they do things differently there.
>   So I tried to get the best of both worlds: I hinted at the possession of hidden treasure, but I did not say what it was.
>
> L. P. Hartley, Prologue
> to *The Go-Between* (1953)

Similarly, a colon can announce or introduce:

> What I really wished to say to you was: I have spoken to the unhappy young woman my daughter . . . .
>
> Evelyn Waugh, *Decline and Fall* (1928)

2   It balances two antithetical parts of a statement:

> To err is human: to forgive divine.
> Alexander Pope, *An Essay*
> *on Criticism* (1711) l. 525

3   As in these examples, it may be used to introduce quotations more than a handful of words
long.

One sometimes still sees colon-plus-dash to introduce a quotation or list, particularly one that starts
on the line below: this practice is unsightly and
unnecessary.

Anthony Powell eccentrically uses the colon with
uncommon liberality, often for no evident purpose:

> In due course, though not before the end of the
> term had been reached, Le Bas agreed to some
> sort of a compromise about the train: Templer
> admitting that he had been wrong in not retur-
> ning earlier . . . .
> *A Question of Upbringing* (1951) ch. 1

Note: American usage requires a colon in the salutation of a letter (*Dear John:*) where British prefers a
comma or nothing.

SEMI-COLON

The semi-colon, increasingly written now as *semicolon*, divides one part of a sentence from another more emphatically than does a comma but without the antithetical dimension of a colon; the elements that it parts, though grammatically distinct, are elements of a single notion.

But towns were rare; they passed not more than one in every four-and-twenty hours.
Vita Sackville-West, *Seducers in Ecuador* (1922)

Semi-colons may occur between clauses or other word groups, and even between single words, particularly where there is an effect of accumulation:

Islets and rocks stained the shield of water; mountains swept down and trod the sea; cities of Illyria rose upon the breast of the coastline; rose; drew near; and faded past.

Ibid.

The sky over London was glorious, ochre and madder, as though a dozen tropic suns were simultaneously setting round the horizon; everywhere the searchlights clustered and hovered, then swept apart; here and there pitchy clouds drifted and billowed; now and then a huge flash momentarily froze the serene fireside glow.

> Evelyn Waugh, *Officers and Gentlemen* (1955) ch. 1

Commas would clearly be inadmissible here, and although full stops would be technically acceptable the effect in both passages would be seriously weakened if they were used. Calculations of technical correctness are not the only ones to be made in choosing between comma and semi-colon in sentences such as these:

I knew she would be late, and she was.
I knew she would be late; and she was.

(The full stop is also a possibility here of course.) A semi-colon may also give a sense of the progression of an argument:

Truth is, indeed, not often welcome for its own sake; it is generally unpleasing because contrary to our wishes and opposite to our practice; and as our attention naturally follows our interest, we hear unwillingly what we are afraid to know . . . .

> Samuel Johnson, *The Rambler*, no. 96 (1751)

Semi-colons are used in preference to commas when a list has items which are lengthy or already divided by commas:

'Shoes, brown, one pair; socks, fancy, one pair; suspenders, black silk, one pair,' read out the warder in a sing-song voice.

Evelyn Waugh, *Decline and Fall* (1928) III.i

Lastly, those who know grammar will note that the semi-colon may divide a sequence of subordinate clauses which are dependent on the same main verb:

It was vehemently argued that this mode of conveyance would be fatal to the breed of horses and to the noble art of horsemanship; that the Thames, which had long been an important nursery of seamen, would cease to be the chief thoroughfare from London up to Windsor and down to Gravesend; that numerous inns at which mounted travellers had been in the habit of stopping would be deserted, and would no longer pay any rent . . .

Sir Thomas Macaulay, quoted in
Frederick T. Wood, *Current English Usage*,
rev. edn (1981) p. 210

COMMA

comma] *the least of the marks of punctuation, and therefore a type of something small and insignificant.*
Samuel Johnson, *A Dictionary of the English Language* (1755)

Joseph Robertson in *An Essay on Punctuation* (1795) gave ten rules for the placing of the comma. This is either too many or too few. The legitimate uses of the comma are many, various, and occasionally subtle, so there would have to be quite a lot of this section even if it were not also the case that the comma is currently, jointly with the apostrophe, the most ill-used mark in our punctuation system. This is partly because there seems to be a widespread ignorance or disregard of sentence structure, and partly because use of the comma is, *within limits*, a matter of personal preference. Some of the limits are described below.

1   A comma may replace *and* in a series of nouns, adjectives or clauses:

Hull, Hell and Halifax.

She was young, blonde and gorgeously impressionable.

George entered the tap-room, looked cautiously around, saw Hughie, and made for the bar.

There are qualifications to this use, however. It is not necessarily the case, for example, that a comma will always separate adjectives. Although we would write a lovable, black-haired terrier

a bright, blue-eyed child

a poor, broken-backed old woman

no commas should appear in

a great big dog

a pretty little girl

a poor old woman*

The reason for this is that commas should only be used when the adjectives are co-ordinate, i.e. when they are of equal weight and each is saying something distinct about the noun (a test for this is to ask whether *and* can successfully be introduced between them). In our first trio of examples there would be no problem putting in an *and* ('a lovable and black-haired terrier'). In the second trio, that is not so, because *great big* is essentially a single concept and has the force of a *compound* adjective,

---

* A radio announcer recently revived the habits of Peter Quince when declaring that a programme would 'return at its new-regular time': was this 'a new, regular time' (i.e. one now having a fixed point in the schedules) or 'a new regular time' (as opposed to the *old* regular time)? Similarly, a misplaced comma in the *Cambridge Guide to Literature in English* (ed. Ian Ousby, Cambridge, 1988) manages to re-write the plot of *Pride and Prejudice*: 'The Bennet family is visited by William Collins, a rector under the patronage of Lady Catherine de Bourgh, who will inherit Mr Bennet's entailed property on his death'.

and in the last examples *little girl* and *old woman* have the force of compound nouns: a *little girl* is a single entity. This is not to say, of course, that there cannot be occasions when such combinations do *not* form single entities and therefore will rely on commas. *Poor old* and *pretty little* have themselves tended to become fixed combinations, but there is a difference between

By then he was a lonely, poor, old man.

and

By then he was rich but very lonely – poor old man.

Other examples: 'the picturesque half-timbered buildings of Stratford', 'the traditional oak panelling', 'this bloody big dog'. A reviewer in the *Times Literary Supplement* in 1985 took John Updike to task for his use, in *The Witches of Eastwick*, of 'a device patented by Saul Bellow, the unpunctuated string of adjectives', and quoted in support of his criticisms 'the ruthless jubilant lucid minds' and 'melancholy triumphant affectionate feelings'. A correspondent retorted that Bellow must in turn have wrested the patent from Henry James, and quoted from the *The Ambassadors* 'a pleasant public familiar radiance', 'strong young grizzled crop' and 'new long smooth avenue'. Here there are similarities with the comma's use with adverbs:

He ran fast and furiously down the road. ·

Suddenly and discordantly, the bell broke the scholars' slumber.

Prepositions and conjunctions likewise:

For George, as for Viv, the birth of baby Julia had something miraculous about it.

Licence my roaving hands, and let them go,
Before, behind, between, above, below . . .
John Donne, 'Elegie XIX'

However, if it is not inconvenient, I shall call again tomorrow.

The current tendency to drop the comma used after conjunctions is to be regretted and occasionally deplored; this is particularly the case with *however*:

However, hard as it may seem, that is the rule.

However hard he works, he has little hope of passing.

Sentences with several conjunctions bring fundamental issues to light.

I hardly like to mention this but if you can see your way to it I'd be grateful for the return of my tenner.

Extreme minimalists would tend to leave this as it appears here; those of the minimalist tendency would settle for a comma before *but*. Others would also put one after *but*, which means there has to be one after *it*. These versions are possible:

(a) I hardly like to mention this, but if you can see your way to it I'd be grateful for the return of my tenner.

(b) I hardly like to mention this, but if you can see your way to it, I'd be grateful for the return of my tenner.

(c) I hardly like to mention this, but, if you can see your way to it, I'd be grateful for the return of my tenner.

(a) is neat and clean; I'd settle for that. (b) makes sense on neither the elocutionary nor the syntactic principle. (c) is faithful to the structure of the sentence and, given the subject matter, manages to suggest something of the diffidence and embarrassment felt by the speaker (though such an abundance of commas might, in other circumstances, merely irritate the reader). Compare

Maureen was a heroine of the struggle, but, awfully, well, *emergent* in her relation to phallo-centrism.

Andrew Davies, *A Very Peculiar Practice* (1986)

In other words, a comma may separate single words, phrases or clauses, but has no place between two grammatically independent sentences that should be parted by a semi-colon or full stop.

Some examples of the 'comma splice':

He didn't get the grades he needed, it means he'll probably resit the exams next year. (Better: *needed, which means.*) Positive discrimination is supposed to achieve equal opportunities for minorities, if it is, then I'm against it. (Better: *minorities; if it is.*)

And from the *Independent* (17 August 1988):

May I pay tribute to my colleagues, they worked long and hard . . .

Another place where a comma should not be seen but often is is at the end of a long subject:

The principal weakness shown in the work of many younger writers who have had no formal training in the disciplines of language, is that they bung in a comma when they shouldn't.

This pause for breath is contrary to the logic and structure of the sentence. Its use is welcome, indeed necessary, in sentences such as this one, where pairs of judgements are given (and compare 'It is likely that most, if not all, of the candidates will pass with flying colours'). The absolute construction can be a handy device ('Susan having finished her jobs for the day, the supervisor let her leave early') but is frequently made a hash of ('Susan, having finished her jobs for the day, the supervisor let her leave early').

2   Difficulties arise in the matter of using a comma before *and*. Simple cases first. Two simple terms joined by *and* (this is true also with *or* and *et cetera*) need no comma:

bread and butter

hell or high water

magazines, papers, books etc.

With three or more items a comma is required before the final *and* if there is danger of misunderstanding. Compare

tea, scones and cake

tea, bread and butter, and cake

The issue here is whether or not the final *and* is conjunctive (i.e. makes a connection) or disjunctive (i.e. introduces a related but separate item). There may be times when you need to punctuate on the model *A, B, and C* rather than *A, B and C* to make clear that *B* and *C*, though related, are not connected:

Laurel and Hardy, and Charlie Chaplin

rather than

Laurel and Hardy and Charlie Chaplin.

This enumerative use needs careful handling in a construction such as 'the finesse of Matthews, the power of Maradona, and the beautiful Pele'; without a comma before this *and* we are attributing power to Pele – which is not the emphasis we want to give here. A final caution on enumeration: 'In the kitchen, omelettes, souffles and meringues, in particular have a way of turning out disastrously.' The comma after *meringues* makes it clear that all three of these items are regarded as disaster-prone; without it the meringue would stand alone as particularly unreliable.

Writing can become messy when commas used for apposition ('Shakespeare, the Swan of Avon') are used in close proximity to commas of enumeration:

Shakespeare, the Swan of Avon, and Johnson, the Swan of Lichfield, the Great Cham and author of the *English Dictionary* would probably be amazed as well as impressed, like the rest of us, by a work such as *A Comprehensive Grammar of the English Language* by Professor Sir Randolph Quirk, President of the British Academy, Sidney Greenbaum, Professor of English Language in the University of London, Jan Svartvik and Professor Geoffrey Leech.

The solution is brackets or, better, a complete re-think.

A similar difficulty arises with co-ordinating clauses. There is not much difficulty with *but*. Fairly short sentences do not need a comma:

He was tired but wanted to press on.

In longer ones a comma is advisable, particularly if there are *and*-clauses in the sentence, or the subject changes:

His father noticed that his son was tired and urged him to finish for the night, but John wanted to press on and get the job done.

With *and*-clauses it can be more difficult. The simplest type is this:

He cleared his desk and went home.

The dog sped up the stairs and occupied the
landing.

No comma here. These sentences have the same
subject in each clause. What if this were not so?

He cleared his desk and Anne waited outside.

The dog sped up the stairs and the cat hardly
stirred.

Until recently fundamentalists would have insisted
(and maybe still would) on a comma before each
and. Is there loss of clarity, or risk of confusion
without one?

He cleared his desk and the office
staff prepared the evening's mail.

In such a case (and particularly if the lay-out
contributes to the effect), the lack of a comma is
likely to trip up the continuity of the reader's
attention.

On occasion there is a further reason to use a
comma in these circumstances.

He was pleased with the work but no one took
much notice of it.

He was pleased with the work, but no one took much notice of it.

The father welcomed publicity at any time but the son was more reticent.
The father welcomed publicity at any time, but the son was more reticent.

In these examples the difference made by the comma is to emphasise the contrast between the paired clauses. Length can be a factor:

The father was something of an outrageous self-publicist who welcomed any opportunity to make himself and his doings better known to a wider range of people, but the son had a horror even of well-intentioned inquiries about his opinions and intentions.

One would have to be a minimalist to the verge of derangement not to include a comma before this *but*. Compare

There had been successive swings from the arbirtrary exercise of power by the Crown to the arbitrary exercise of power by Parliament, and the Glorious Revolution had the effect of establishing a stable understanding of the constitutional rights and functions of both.

Where it is a case not of co-ordinate clauses but

of main and subordinate, some latitude of practice is allowable. Consider the following groups of sentences.

(a)   She resigned at the earliest opportunity.

      She resigned because she was bored.

      She had known him since they had gone up to Oxford together.

Other things being equal, a comma in these sentences is not needed and would be distracting.

(b)   As soon as he got in, he poured himself a drink.

      Because he thinks me a rival, he has become much less friendly to me.

      Since she arrived in Oxford, she has been a more confident but less likeable person.

A comma here is not essential but very helpful. This is even more the case with longer sentences:

(c)   After all the disturbance and heartache that family has had to endure, it is a joy to see them having some good luck for a change.

      Whatever Mary has to say, and when the

Senior Tutor has stuck his oar in, it is still a matter, fundamentally, of where the incident took place, and why, and who saw it.

A courteous as well as a careful writer will always be aware of, and guided by, a sense of the reader's convenience – which did not happen in these instances, where commas would have helped after *place*, *So* and *thinking*:

Queer old place this . . . .
Evelyn Waugh, *Officers and Gentlemen* (1955) I.6

So fitfully sleeping and thinking he passed the hours until reveille.
Waugh, *Men at Arms* (1952) II.5

3 Correct use of commas is crucial in defining and non-defining clauses. A defining clause specifies and uses no comma; a non-defining clause supplies extra material (and could be omitted) and requires a pair of commas. Compare

(a)   The girl, who came yesterday, is called Anne
(b)   *The girl who came yesterday is called Anne.*

(a)   The terrace, which overlooks the park, was a favourite haunt of lovers.
(b)   *The terrace which overlooks the park was a favourite haunt of lovers.*

In each of these pairs sentence (a) is non-defining, and (b) defining.

4   Most uses of the comma in apposition are straightforward:

Tony Hilton, best man at my wedding, is himself a bachelor.

Anthony Burgess, that most prolific of writers, has another one out this week.

However, even here there is scope for nuance.

(a)   My cousin, Mary Spencer, is an excellent needlewoman.
(b)   *My cousin Mary Spencer is an excellent needle-woman.*

(a)   means that I have only one cousin; she is called Mary Spencer and is good with a needle.
(b)   means that of the many cousins in my extensive family it is Mary who is the needlewoman. (The almost universal American practice of dispensing with commas in such a case loses this nuance.)

5   We have seen that it is no longer the done thing to follow the example of this sentence from *Little Dorrit* and the one following:

A further remarkable thing in this little old

woman was, that she had no name but Mr F's aunt.

He said, that nothing gave him more pleasure.

In an indirect statement of this kind the comma is dropped. In *direct* speech, however, it is essential, particularly if (as sometimes happens) no inverted commas are used:

He said, Nothing gives me more pleasure.

Nothing gives me more pleasure, he said.

Nothing, he said, gives me more pleasure.

This seems an unnecessary and unhelpful way of dealing with direct speech (see 'Inverted commas').

Summary

I have nothing to say concerning the use of the comma in figures or in correspondence (except to note a growing tendency not to use it in salutation, subscription or addresses), but briefly indicate some of its other uses, which often overlap or are implied in the longer treatment above. Some illustrative sentences then follow.

1   *Adverbial clauses* (particularly longer ones)

(a) CONCESSIVE:

Although she is a brute, he loves her to madness.

However often he rang, she was never at home to him.

(b) CONDITIONAL:

If you have the time to help, I'd appreciate it.

(c) TEMPORAL:

Whenever they find an opportunity to be alone, they take it.

(d) SPATIAL:

Where the bus stops, there shop I.

(e) CAUSAL:

Because of the fall in the value of the pound, her holiday turned out to be unexpectedly expensive.

(Note that a comma is generally better dispensed with after *therefore* – certainly at the beginning of a sentence, unless the sentence begins with something appositional or in other ways subordinate.)

2 *Appeal*

Oh night, which ever art when day is not!
> Shakespeare, *A Midsummer
> Night's Dream*, v.i.168

Oh! Sophonisba! Sophonisba! Oh!
> James Thomson, *Sophonisba*, iii.ii

O Julius Caesar! thou art mighty yet!
> Shakespeare, *Julius Caesar*, v.iii.94

Down, Shep! Kiss me, you silly boy.

Note. The convention regarding *O* and *Oh* used to be that *O* is used for the vocative (as in *O mighty Caesar!*) and when the sound is to be understood as closely associated with what follows, and not marked off from it (as in *O for the wings of a dove*); *Oh*, on the other hand, is an independent exclamation, marked off from what follows by a comma or exclamation mark (as in *Oh, crumbs!* or *Oh, how fleeting are the joys of youth*). It is a convention it would do no harm to keep.

3 *Adversative*

On the other hand, I quite like Verdi.

4 *Assent and dissent*

Yes, I do. No, you don't.

5 *Dates.* It is best to keep the numbers apart, then there is no need for commas: *31 December 1999* rather than *December 31, 1999.*

6 *Parenthetical*

They knew that, with the licensing laws as they were, by the time they got out of *Hamlet*, being as long as it was, there would be no chance of their getting a drink.

7 *Participial*

Being a serious drinker, he vowed never again to go to a *Hamlet* or a *Lear.*

Philip, engrossed in the intricacies of his paper-work, lost all track of the time.

8 *Interrogative tags*

You love him, don't you?

It's tomorrow, isn't it?

9 *Polite forms*

Two singles, please.

Not for me, thank you.

10 *Vocative*

Come in, Mary,

Not now, Peter.

And note: *University College, Oxford; University College London.*

Prudent readers will have always in mind the caution given by Poe:

> Even when the sense is perfectly clear, a sentence may be deprived of half its force – its spirit – its point – by improper punctuation. For the want of merely a comma, it often occurs that an axiom appears a paradox, or that sarcasm is converted into a sermonoid.
>
> Edgar Allan Poe, *Marginalia* (1844–9)

It is a braver man than I that would seem to disagree with Pope, who, it will be remembered, held it against some of his many critics that:

> Commas and points they set exactly right,
> And 'twere a sin to rob them of their mite.
> 'Prologue to the Satires' (1735) ll.161–2

As a warning (or reassurance) that even the best can sometimes get it wrong, here are two sentences from Hardy's *Jude the Obscure* (1896):

When he entered Sue, who had been keeping indoors during his absence, laid out supper for him.   (v.2)

A few days after a figure moved through the white fog which enveloped the Beersheba suburb of Christminster, towards the quarter in which Jude Fawley had taken up his lodging since his division from Sue.   (vɪ.4)

The sentences that follow have been chosen to illustrate some of the uses of the comma (and of the colon and semi-colon); but they have not been chosen with an eye to technical correctness only, and readers may like to consider the differences of effect and of suggestion that would have resulted from alternative uses.

Wretched in spirit, groaning under the feeling of the insult, self-condemning, and ill-satisfied in every way, Bold returned to his London lodgings. Ill as he had fared in his interview with the archdeacon, he was not the less under the necessity of carrying out his pledge to Eleanor; and he went about his ungracious task with a heavy heart.

> Anthony Trollope, *The Warden* (1855) ch. 7

Yet plenty, after all, remained alive; and these, having given thanks for their preservation, mingled in a grand passagio up and down the terrace which overlooked the 1st XI cricket ground.

Simon Raven, *Fielding Gray* (1969)

Merton Densher, who passed the best hours of each night at the office of his newspaper, had at times, during the day, to make up for it, a sense, or at least an appearance, of leisure, in accordance with which he was infrequently to be met, in different parts of the town, at moments when men of business are hidden from the public eye.

Henry James, *The Wings of the Dove* (1902) ch. 3

Aunt Gertrude, too tight perm, awkward feet in too tight shoes, grasping a shiny, patent leather handbag like the week's groceries. Melanie remembered the Ashes of Violet flavoured kisses of her Aunt Gertrude from the few family Christmases when grandfather (scowling at the camera as if he expected it to gobble his soul) was alive. Good-bye, Grandfather. Good-bye, Auntie Gertrude.

Angela Carter, *The Magic Toyshop* (1961) ch. 1

Slowly, amidst almost intolerable noises from, on the one hand, the street and, on the other, from the large and voluminously echoing play-

ground, the depths of the telephone began, for
Valentine, to assume an aspect that, years ago,
it had used to have – of being a part of the
supernatural paraphernalia of inscrutable
Destiny.

Ford Madox Ford, *A Man Could
Stand Up* (1926) ch. 1

She reclined against my shoulder while I exam-
ined a tress of her dark hair, surprised again to
find in it so many threads of a pure reddish gold.
Her hair was as straight as a horse's tail, almost
as coarse, and very long.

Iris Murdoch, *A Severed Head* (1961) ch. 1

Feeling a tremendous rakehell, and not liking
myself much for it, and feeling rather a good
chap for not liking myself much for it, and not
liking myself at all for feeling rather a good chap,
I got indoors, vigorously rubbing lipstick off my
mouth with my handkerchief. This would form
the sole item in a little private wash-day some
time to-morrow; Jean used a different shade.

Kingsley Amis, *That Uncertain
Feeling* (1955) ch. 7

There were two dry, empty sea-urchins; two
rusty magnets, a large one and a small one,
which had almost lost their magnetism; some
negatives rolled up in a tight coil; some stumps
of sealing-wax; a small combination lock with

three rows of letters; a twist of very fine whip-cord, and one or two ambiguous objects, of which the use was not at once apparent: I could not even tell what they had belonged to.

L. P. Hartley,
Prologue to *The Go-Between* (1953)

So he ate an orange, slowly spitting out the seeds. Outside, the snow was turning to rain. Inside, the electric stove seemed to give no heat and rising from his writing-table, he sat down upon the stove. How good it felt! Here, at least, was life.

Ernest Hemingway, 'Banal Story',
Men without Women (1928)

Then I saw the raging sea, and the rollers tumbling in on the sand-bank, and the driven rain sweeping over the waters like a flying garment, and the yellow wilderness of the beach with one solitary black figure standing on it – the figure of Sergeant Cuff.

Wilkie Collins, *The Moonstone* (1868)
First Period, ch. 19

Though they are not, strictly speaking, stops but tones, it will be convenient to deal here with the question mark and the exclamation mark (in the United States more commonly *interrogation point* and *exclamation point*). Each of these is formed of a mark made above a full stop or period. The upper part of the question mark may be thought of as representing a *q*, an abbreviated form of Latin *quaere*, imperative of *quaerere* ('to ask'); alternatively it may be an inversion of the Greek interrogation mark (;). The upper part of the exclamation mark has a pointer, or dagger, overhanging the dot. The Dutch scholar Bilderdijk suggested that ? is formed of the *q* and *o* of Latin *quaestio* ('question'), with the *o* eventually reducing to a dot; similarly he takes ! to be the Latin *Io* (an exclamation of joy or triumph), the *I* being set over the *o*, which again reduces to a dot.[1]

QUESTION MARK

1 A question mark comes (and should come) at the end of a direct question:

Do you come here often?

It does not come at the end of an indirect question;

I asked her if she came here often.

Compare

Where is she? I ask myself.

Where could she be, I wondered.

Where it might all end he did not care to imagine.

As a rule, of course, a question is also signified by inverting the order of subject and verb, but any word order that has the *effect* of a question requires a question mark. Compare

You like her.

You like her? (Also: *You* like her? You *like* her? You like *her*?)

2 By the same token, questions that are not really questions (but expressions of surprise, anger and so on) do not take the mark:

Who should be there but Kath!

What has he been up to now!

The selection or omission of an exclamation mark in these expressions will be determined by the context, as with expressions such as *Would you believe it* and *What do you know*.

In England now *How d'ye do* is not a question, and those people should be locked up who tell you (usually at some length) how they are when what you have said to them is *How are you!* (greeting), not *How are you?* (question).

3 Similarly, what appear to be questions but are

simply polite forms allow but do not require the mark:

May I ask you to pass the port?

When you have completed the questionnaire, will you be so good as to return it in the pre-paid envelope provided.

In the first example here, which clearly relates to something said, it is advisable to retain the mark as an indication of rising intonation, and all the more so if all that is said is *Port, please*? or even *Port*?; in the second, written, example, there is clearly no need.

Could there, unknown to him, have been anyone else in the house at the time? No, he was sure there couldn't. Could anyone, during the morning, have entered or left by the back way? No again. Certain? Certain.

> Simon Raven, *Fielding Gray* (1969)

As always, though, if it is genuinely interrogative instead of merely seeming so, the mark is needed:

May I see you again?

May I have this dance?

(To be genuinely interrogative, these examples might require a slight emphasis on *may*.)

4 Some care is needed with what are commonly called 'rhetorical questions'. It is important to distinguish cases that call for a simple full stop or exclamation mark from those that call for a question mark. Compare

How good were the good old days?

How good Winnie always was to me.

What nonsense to talk of 'minimalist punctuation'! is clearly an exclamation, an expression of a point of view; *What wonder readers get confused with all this minimalist punctuation* might be again an exclamation, or it might be an elliptical form of the question *What wonder is it*? requiring a question mark.

As with all these things, the crucial matters are the real meaning of the words and the reader's convenience. So, despite the warning about indirect questions given above, there will be occasons when it will be quite proper to write

I wonder if Margaret has remembered that we're going there tonight?

Given the scope for misunderstanding here – getting to the end of a sentence before realising you have been reading a question – there does seem sense in the Spanish convention of placing a question mark (whichever way up) at the start of the sentence. The use of a bracketed question mark to suggest incredulity or scorn should be avoided: 'he had never been convinced of the benefits (?) of a vegetarian diet'.

EXCLAMATION MARK

Here there is almost more to say about abuse than use.

1 This mark is used after interjections, or words that have the force of interjections, and after any words intended to express sounds that are loud, sudden or powerful. Readers will know plenty of these, some of them not fit to print: *Crash!, Bang!, Good God!, Ouch!*

As with the question mark, careful writers will attend to the meaning and context of the words, not just to their apparent form, so

(a) when words such as *bang* and *crash* are not interjectional they require no mark:

The crash of the vase as it fell into the hearth woke grandfather from his doze.

(b) although a verb may be in the imperative, a mark is required only if the word is to be understood as uttered in an exclamatory tone (*Halt! Who goes there?*); it is not required in *Sleep now, baby*.

(c) even though an expression may be exclamatory in form, it will require a mark only if it is exclamatory in meaning also. (Compare what was said above about rhetorical questions.) There is a clear difference between these two examples:

What is that woman doing?

What is that woman doing!

Compare also

What a fool you are, Giles!

What a shame you didn't know before you left Rome.

2 The exclamation mark is to be used also in the device known as *apostrophe* (or invocation):

Milton! thou shouldst be living at this hour.
William Wordsworth, 'London, 1802'

This is different from the less intense vocative, which requires only a comma:

All hail, Macbeth! Hail to thee, Thane of Glamis!
Shakespeare, *Macbeth*, i.iii.47

3 *Occasionally* the mark may be used at the end of a sentence to indicate a note of surprise, dismay, astonishment, distaste or other strong feeling. It should always be used in accordance with the context (so what is genuinely a question – for example, *How on earth did you manage*? – should have a question mark, not an exclamation mark). Above all, it should certainly be used sparingly, even frugally, few things being more tiresome than the spray of exclamation marks used by writers who use it as a 'mark of admiration'. It is a certain sign of weak writing that this mark is overused to impart a factitious effectiveness beyond the power of the writer's meagre talents. It is an affliction endemic in certain kinds of study guide (*Imagine Pip's amazement when he sees it's Estella again!*), advertising bumf, and the more 'uplifting' kinds of religious literature.

Multiple exclamation marks are best left to schoolchildren and those in love for the first time:

'Played Lambton House At Home. Match Drawn 1–1.' 'Played Lambton House Away. Match Drawn 3–3.' Then, 'Last and Ultimate and Final Replay. Lambton House VANQUISHED 2–1!!!! McClintock scored both goals!!!!'

L. P. Hartley,
Prologue to *The Go-Between* (1953)

'It was true, wasn't it? Besides I put an exclamation mark to show.'

'Show what?'

'That it wasn't serious. The nuns never minded if you put an exclamation mark. "Mother Superior in a tearing rage!" They always called it the "exaggeration mark".'

Graham Greene,
A Burnt-Out Case (1960) vi.2

John Fowles in *The French Lieutenant's Woman* whimsically takes himself to task for overdoing the exclamation marks, and Gerard Manley Hopkins uses the mark sixteen times in the first eleven lines of his poem 'The Starlight Night'.

Similarly the mixture of exclamation and question marks is best left to comics and *Private Eye*:

Nigel Lawson! Don't ya love him!!!???!!!

Both exclamation and question marks take the place of full stops at the end of a sentence:

As soon as we had climbed into the hayloft, he had looked at me redly, as if to say, 'What now?'

Simon Raven, *Fielding Gray* (1969)

Within a sentence they supersede any mark that would otherwise have occurred in their place, and in these circumstances are only followed by a capital letter if the next word would take one anyway:

This is the very he, forsooth! I am to marry.

Their place in relation to inverted commas will be discussed under that heading. So there!

That punctuation can communicate without the presence of words is shown by this passage from A. A. Milne's *Winnie the Pooh*:

'We might go in your umbrella,' said Pooh.
'?'
'We might go in your umbrella,' said Pooh.
'??'
'We might go in your umbrella,' said Pooh.
'!!!!!!'
For suddenly Christopher Robin saw that they might.

Some people's oral style is more obviously punctuational than others'. Consider this comment by Ned Sherrin in the *Radio Times* (7–13 January 1989):

David Frost is still a formidable inquisitor when his mind is engaged by the subject or when his nose scents skulduggery and he has time to do his homework. In these circumstances his sentences lose the feeling of being composed of phrases encased in quotes, prefaced by stage directions as to how they should be delivered and followed by an exclamation mark.

A NOTE ON PRETTY WHILES

The idea that these stops relate to periods of time, to pauses in delivery, is an old one, but a mistaken one. The earliest English exposition of it is given by Ben Jonson (*c.*1617):

There resteth one generall affection of the whole [of Syntaxe], disposed thorow every member thereof, as the bloud is thorow the body; and consisteth in the breathing, when we pronounce any *Sentence*; For, whereas our breath is by nature so short, that we cannot continue without a stay to speake long together; it was thought necessarie, as well for the speakers ease, as for the plainer deliverance of the things spoken, to invent this meanes, whereby men, pausing a pretty while, the whole speech might never the worse be understood.

> *The English Grammar Made by*
> *Ben Jonson* (published 1640)

Jonson's explicit assumption is that the purpose of

punctuation is to facilitate reading aloud, and therefore the stops – as well as allowing readers to breathe – tell them *when* to breathe. But for how long? How long is a pretty while? Lindley Murray (*English Grammar*, 1795) offers a classic definition of relative prettiness which was still current, in essence, thirty years ago:

> The Comma represents the shortest pause; the Semicolon, a pause double that of the comma; the Colon, double that of the semicolon; and the Period, double that of the colon.

Acknowledging that 'the precise quantity or duration of each pause, cannot be defined', he nevertheless insists that 'the proportion between the pauses should be ever invariable'. (See frontispiece.)

Whatever the time intervals may be, can anyone conceive of a piece of writing so subtle, so finely calculated, that its effectiveness requires pauses marked with this degree of mathematical precision? Who needs two intervals of pause between a comma and a full stop? (And how long should you pause for a bracket?) This is not to decry the crucial importance of using the marks correctly and with discernment. Archbishop Temple (1938): 'Intellectually, stops matter a great deal. If you are getting your commas, semi-colons, and full stops wrong, it means that you are not getting your thoughts right, and your mind is muddled.'[2] This is absolutely right, and should re-route our attention to the fact that modern punctuation is related to syntax, and is to that extent functional rather than expressive. The 'pretty while' principle operates on two mistaken ideas. The first is the failure to recognise that speech and writing are two quite separate language systems requiring different rules and conventions. The second is the belief that commas and so on can be a suitable guide to performance, but with no note taken of pitch, pace, volume and other factors that would need to be marked for a written text to work like a musical score. That is a laudable, if probably impossible, system to hope for, but it is not the purpose of the system we've got. Compare the comments by Sir Ralph Richardson:

> In music the punctuation is absolutely strict, the bars and the rests are absolutely defined, but our [that is, actors'] punctuation cannot be quite strict, because we have to relate to the audience. In other words, we are continually changing the score.[3]

3

Dashes, Dots and Flying Commas

Apostrophe – brackets – dashes and dots – hyphen – inverted commas

APOSTROPHE

> *What kind of a piano* is *this – no apostrophes!!*
> Jimmy Durante, 'The Man Who Found
> the Lost Chord' (song)

We took the mark from the French and the word, via Latin, from the Greek ἡ ἀπόστροφος προσωδία ('he apostrophos prosodia'), the accent of turning away – i.e. of elision or omission. (Also from the verb *apostrophein* is the rhetorical figure of the same name that denotes a 'turning away' to address, as it might be, the moon or Destiny.) In my primary school it was known as 'the flying comma'.

The apostrophe has two major functions and a range of minor ones. These all seem fairly straightforward but are so frequently got wrong, even by people who are otherwise quite bright and literate, that one sometimes wonders if it is worth persevering with. In a number of cases the apostrophe is starting to be dropped anyway, and the notes that follow indicate some examples of where it has outlived its usefulness.

Omission

An apostrophe is used to indicate that some letter or letters have been omitted in forming a shortened version of a word or phrase, including all reduced verb forms: *isn't* (and the maverick *ain't*), *'Fraid not, Middlesboro', ten o'clock, cat i'th'window, ne'er-do-well.* Generally if letters are omitted at more than one place, only the second omission is marked, as in *shan't*. In *plane* (for *aeroplane*), *bus* and *phone* an opening apostrophe will now seem unduly fussy. Omission of figures may be signified this way also – *'69* for *1969* (or whatever century is involved) – and is so signified, especially in denoting vintages. Some contemporary uses are to be deplored, but we are probably stuck with them: *Rock'n'Roll* was all right, but there is now too much *his'n'hers* and its equivalents, and far too much *kiss'n'tell*.

The apostrophe goes where the omission has been made; a home-brew supplies shop near where

I live calls itself SOMETHI'N BREWI'N. Compare

> Behind these was an unlit building with a painted
> sign, faintly visible, reading *Car's for hire* –
> *Batesons* – *Repair's*.
>
> Kingsley Amis, *Lucky Jim* (1954) ch. 14

Possession

The possessive apostrophe also was originally a
mark of omission, since it showed the dropping of
the *e* in words such as *foxes* (*the foxes tail*). The
apostrophe appears in a number of uses of the
English genitive, chiefly to show possession. If Ben
Jonson in his *English Grammar* (written 1617 but not
published until 1640) knew about the apostrophe
of omission, 'the rejecting of a vowell from the
beginning or ending of a word', the apostrophe of
possession was still unknown to him. Jonson would
write 'The mad Doggs foame' just as Chaucer wrote
The Clerkes Tale, and Elizabethan and Jacobean
literature abounds in expressions built on the model
of *Mr Jones his book* and *the prince his house*. (How
we got from *John his book* to *John's book* or *Anne her
book* to *Anne's book* is far from clear; in Dutch they
didn't follow this course, and have retained a
distinct feminine form which is literally, 'Anne of
her the book'.) The first showing of the apostrophe
was to indicate to readers the basic form of a
possibly unfamiliar word: Milton (died 1674) has

mans but *Siloa's brook* to show that the basic form is *Siloa*. Our *'s* form emerged in about 1680 to denote possessive singular, and the possessive plural *s'* form did not appear until a century or so later.

To judge by the tucks they get themselves into, many people would be just as happy if possession apostrophes had never appeared at all. Yet the rules governing their use are quite simple and, as English rules go, remarkably exception-free. There is certainly some latitude in the use of accompaniments to the possession apostrophe (notably in the matter of adding an extra *s* or not), but the rules about where the apostrophe goes are quite clear. The infallible way to get this right is to understand that the apostrophe immediately follows the name of the possessor (only one exception – which we'll come to later). So,

Andrew's pen is the pen of *Andrew*

Louise's book is the book of *Louise*

An equally certain recipe for disaster is to think the apostrophe 'goes before the *s*'. Sometimes it seems to, but that is merely an accident of English forms. Apply that mistaken rule and you end with nonsense such as *Keat's* poems (or the poems of *Keat*), the *princes's* or *prince'ss* tiara, and what do you do with *Jesus*?

Although it ends with *s*, *James* is treated exactly

the same as *Andrew* in our example above:

James's pen is the pen of *James*

So, it's *Henry James's novels, Charles Dickens's London* and *Tess's ancestral family name of d'Urberville*.

The examples we have considered so far are all singular. Those who are confused become more so when dealing with plurals, particularly with words that complicate matters further by forming a plural with an extra *s*. The rule for placing the apostrophe remains the same.

Singular	Plural	Possessive
twin	twins	the twins' playgroup
priest	priests	the priests' housekeeper
book	books	the books' second-hand value
curtain	curtains	the curtains' faded colours

There is of course a group of words that do not add *s* to form the plural; instead they either change in the middle (e.g. from *man* to *men*) or change near the end (e.g. from *woman* to *women*) or add something (as with *child* and *children*); some do not change at all (*sheep, sheep*), and some, already ending in single or double *s*, add *es* (*crosses, Joneses*). Through all these variations of plural formation the rule for the apostrophe of possession does not change; the apostrophe still immediately follows the possessor:

Singular	Possessive	Plural	Possessive
man	man's	men	men's hats
woman	woman's	women	women's room
child	child's	children	children's portions
sister	sister's	sisters	the sisters' jealousy
Jones	Jones's	Joneses	the Joneses' house
Princess	Princess's	Princesses	the Princesses' husbands

The possessive case signifies the closest of relationships, at least in a grammatical sense. In a virtuoso display of apostrophe use, Gerard Manley Hopkins, the Victorian poet and priest, pushes, almost to the limits of what is possible, his expression of how close he feels to Christ:

Our heart's charity's hearth's fire, our thought's chivalry's throng's Lord.
The Wreck of the Deutschland (1875) stanza 35

It should now be possible to consider some special cases, but bearing in mind that the rule for the position of the apostrophe still does not change.

1 *Nouns in -nce.* Pronunciation is the key here. If the noun makes a shushing noise (*conscience*, *patience*) then it does not need an extra *s*, so write 'for *insurance*' sake'. Otherwise punctuate as normal, by adding *s* after the apostrophe (*absence's* power to make the heart grow fonder).

2 *Nouns in -ss.* Many of these are proper names and will be dealt with in a separate section; discussion here is confined to common nouns. In the singular the tendency is to add *s* after the apostrophe, but sound is a crucial factor and should almost always be the guide. It is probably safe to write 'the *crisis's* most acute moments', 'the *abscess's* colour' and 'the *consensus's* effectiveness'. Similarly, with nouns in *-ess*, an older style is yielding to a modern preference for 'a *hostess's* duties', 'a *princess's* public role'. (If some of these examples sound a little unidiomatic it is because most people, faced with a problem of this sort, will rightly prefer to recast the sentence.) There is a special case that may arise in speech or in writing representing speech. 'She does not like her daughter's mixing with that crowd' is a perfectly correct sentence which, merely heard, would not make clear how many daughters were involved; punctuation, the art of *written* marks, uncovers all. Again, only punctuation can sort out all the potential ambiguities in dealing with 'one of my son's friends' / 'one of my sons' friends'.

3 *Proper names in -s.* There is a perfectly unobjectionable convention that names from Latin and Greek literature, mythology and history take only an apostrophe; *Odysseus' return; Thucydides' prose style; Xerxes' troops.* This applies also to *Jesus* and forms in *-z* (*Sanchez' marriage, Boaz' wife*). Modern names now generally take an additional *s: Pepys's* *diaries, Adams's irritating book about rabbits.* A special case is that of French names. As pronounced in French and by educated English speakers the *s* is not sounded in names such as *Degas* and *Rabelais.* However, in their possessive forms in English an *s* is clearly heard, and in writing this is taken as being the *s* that already appears as the last letter, and so a further one does not need to be written. This is a long-winded way of telling you to write *Degas' bronzes* and *Rabelais' lively sense of fun.* Ditto with Le Roux and other names in -*x*. For personal names ending in *s* (including Christian names that sometimes are used as surnames) add '*s* if an additional syllable is heard in pronouncing the possessive: *Jones's, Thomas's, Charles's*; otherwise leave well alone: *Mrs Jeffreys' apple-pie.* Family names that sound like the plurals of common nouns do not add anything: *a history of the Trees' amazing careers; tonight we're eating at the Bridges'.*

4 *'Free' genitive.* The last-given example is a reminder of the apostrophe in the 'free' genitive, as in *St Paul's, been to the butcher's/baker's/candlestick-maker's/George's,* where *cathedral/church, house, shop* is understood to be understood. Some houses and clubs that are also effectively genitival dispense with the apostrophe (*Blandings, Stringfellows, Annabels, Brooks*). There is no consensus over *Lord's* or *Lords* (Cricket Ground), the *OED Supplement* giving both.

5 *Group genitives.* The apostrophe signifies an

owner (or author, or inventor or anyone having a claim to the following noun or noun-phrase). Usually this owner is a single item but may be multiple; placing of the apostrophe will depend on whether the 'ownership' is to be considered as separate and individual or as communal and joint. Compare *Clare and Aidan's father* (which means that Clare and Aidan are siblings and that *father* refers to one man) and *Clare's and Aidan's father(s)* (where clearly two men are involved). Some examples will illustrate the point:

William and Mary's accession in 1688

Religious controversy characterised Mary Tudor's and James II's reign. (Better: *reigns.*)

Note also this way of proceeding with items such as

George Duke of Clarence's strange death

The man who came last weekend's coat

The Princess of Wales' engagements for the day

There id an important distinction between *Gilbert and Sullivan's operas* and *Charlotte's and Emily's novels.*

Particular care is needed in the use of possessive

adjectives and possessive pronouns (which never take an apostrophe). Consider

> *Your* and *my* agreement (i.e. our *joint* agreement)

> *Your* and *my* agreements (our separate agreements)

> *Peter's, your* and *my* agreement (our *joint* agreement)

> *Peter's, your* and *my* agreements (three agreements)

> *Peter's* and *your* (*Your* and *Peter's*) agreement (shared)

> *Peter's* and *your* (*Your* and *Peter's*) agreements (separate)

Where the 'agreements' are separate items, it is possible to vary the pattern by introducing the noun after the first possessive adjective:

> *His* agreement and *yours* and *mine*

(though it is of course not clear if this refers to two or three agreements). An apostrophe must not be used with the pronouns *hers, his, its, ours, yours, theirs*.

6   *Genitive compounds.* Close compounds such as *lady's maid* and *bird's egg* may make the plural *lady's maids* or *ladies' maids*, *bird's eggs* or *birds' eggs*. However, in cases where the genitive word must obviously be a plural no leeway is allowable: thus, *birds' nests*. Note also a distinction between such expressions used literally and the like expressions used figuratively: *crows' nests* (literal) but *crow's nests* (on ship); *bulls' eyes* (literal) but *bull's eyes* (both sweets and targets).

7   *Post-genitive.* This is the use of the apostrophe in those odd expressions on the model of *a letter of Byron's, a friend of my father's*.

8   *Abbreviations.* Abbreviations and other short forms are punctuated according to the rule *Elizabeth II's, Sutcliffe and Co's tripe*. (Note that the apostrophe drives out the full stop of abbreviation in *Co.*)

9   *Funny plurals.* By 'funny' is meant words formed *ad hoc* as there is no regular or existing form. This is the case with, for example, individual letters: *Mind your p's and q's; How many f's in 'phosphorus'?* *Betas* and *gammas* probably do not need the apostrophe. *There are four 8's in my phone number.* A comparable case is *arguing the pro's and con's*; in writing this by hand there is no alternative to the apostrophe, but print could get away with italics: *pros* and *cons*. Compare 'What do all these *ibids* mean?' There is neither need nor excuse for shoving an apostrophe into *1940s, MPs*. Consider the *pros* and *cons* in the following examples:

My class has four Tracy's and six Darren's.

All the proud grandpa's and grandma's were there.

These *thou*'s and *forsooth*'s make Shakespeare unreadable.

To a starving French peasant this was an unimaginable sum of *louis's*.

10 *Firms*. This is a Macmillan(s) book, and this sentence illustrates the tendency, perfectly all right, to give companies, firms and publishing-houses an extra *s* with no apostrophe. In some cases the extra *s* has become standard, or nearly so. Compare *Harrods, Lloyds Bank, W. H. Smiths, Debenhams*.

11 *Odds and sods*. The apostrophe has a use in trying to make some exotic words look English, as well as more familiar words when they are used as parts of speech they have never been before. Examples: *mascara* and *henna, beret* and *umbrella*. What is the past tense of *polka? Polka-ed* or *polka'd*? Lawrence Durrell in the *Bafut Beagles* (1954) goes for 'we *polkaed* round the room'. Do you make it one word, use a dash or an apostrophe? Following Durrell's example, it is also *rumbaed* and, amazingly to some eyes, *cha-cha-chaed*? Or *cha-cha-cha'd*? The following examples are all from recent novels, but this issue is still in such a state of uncertainty that, despite the standing of their authors, they cannot be regarded as the last word:

her heavily mascaraed eyelids

with hennaed red hair

the umbrella-ed Mr Steadman

a diamante-ed trouser-suit[1]

Martin Amis too uses *hennaed* (in *Dead Babies*, ch. 28), as he does bikini-ed (ch. 20) and Amis senior's *Difficulties with Girls* (1988) has *crocheted shawls*. Readers may wish to propose their own solutions to the problems posed by, say, *sauté'd* or *purée-ed*, *candelabra'd* or *verandahed*, *arc'd* or *anorak-ed*. The problems are not new. Graham Greene's *A Gun for Sale* (1936) has *villa'd suburbs*, and what solution was ever found to variants of *recce* (abbreviation of *reconnaissance*): *recce'd? recceing?*

The apostrophe also appears, looking odd, in some family names with foreign origins (*De'ath*) and in transciptions from languages with other alphabets *Rubá'iyát of Omar Khayyám*). It occurs in expressions such as *two weeks' holiday* and *two years' imprisonment*. It is often used, illogically and often distractingly, to suggest dialect: for example, in

Wuthering Heights (Yorkshire dialect) and many of the stories of Kipling (Cockney), and in renditions of the speech of the huntin', shootin' an' fishin' set. It does not appear in most place-names where you might expect it, from *St Albans* to *St Kitts* (check with an atlas), but an apostrophe precedes the *s* in

Connah's Quay; Hunter's Quay; Land's End; Orme's Head; The Queen's College (Oxford); St Abb's Head; St John's (Oxford college and Newfoundland); St John's Wood (home of Lord's Cricket Ground); St Michael's Mount; St Mungo's Well.[2]

Note the position of the apostrophe in *Queens' College* (Cambridge).

Where something is *for*, rather than *of*, something, drop the apostrophe: *Womens Institute, Girls School, Students Common Room*; but *The Writers' and Artists' Yearbook 1988* persists with it.

For the same reason we could, in theory, do without it in *mens shoes* – no possession, no omission, and no risk of misunderstanding; see comments on Milton, above. There is no case, however, for moving on from that point to legitimate, say, 'the mens shoes were wet and discoloured after their owners long walk over the sodden hills'. Partly on the grounds that so many people get it wrong, Robert Burchfield and Philip Howard appear to argue for a return to pre-Miltonic innocence, for abandonment of the apostrophe alto-gether.[3] There are three arguments against this. First, items such as *mens, Austens* and *Marys* look un-English, German in fact. Secondly, the answer to people getting it wrong is to teach them to get it right. Thirdly, there is no imagining the further idiocies likely to result from removing an extra control from the language of those who have already shown themselves incapable of operating a simple rule. *Floreat!*

There is no apostrophe in the titles *Howards End* and *Finnegans Wake*.

A *mathematics teacher* is indeed a teacher *of* mathe-matics, but no apostrophe is required as the noun is here used attributively (compare *history teacher*).

The sole exception to the rule for placing the apostrophe, referred to throughout this section, is *its* (= belonging to it), to avoid confusion with *it's* (= it is/has).

We may finish by looking at some cautionary examples drawn from the 'quality' British press:

Some writer's houses have become popular tourist haunts . . . .

Independent, 11 August 1988

A key weakness in the Governments attempt to impose sweeping censorship . . . despite the Lords claim of the right to gag . . . .

Observer, 2 August 1987

They were planning to kidnap Charlotte . . . and hold her for four million francs ransom. . . . They had already robbed a jewellers and a gunsmiths.
Independent, 12 March 1987

Publishers are not immune:

This week Hodder & Stoughton publishes a new book about childrens language, literacy and learning . . . .[4]

BRACKETS

Brackets come in a variety of shapes and, as far as punctuation is concerned, are a device for parenthesis. *Parenthesis* (plural *parentheses*) is derived from Greek words that may be translated as 'a placing-alongside', and what goes into brackets is material that runs along with the main sentence but is not an integral part of it. The three commonest kinds of brackets are round, square and diamond (or angle), and each kind is reserved for different purposes.

Round brackets

Round brackets enclose the letters or numbers that identify elements in a series – (a), (b), (c), (i), (ii), (iii). Words within round brackets may offer

comment or reflection, an afterthought or a reference:

> My lady and Mr Godfrey (not knowing what Mr
> Franklin and I knew) both started, and both
> looked surprised.
>> Wilkie Collins, *The Moonstone* (1868)

> Nuclear war is hard to imagine; but so is nuclear
> disarmament. (Nuclear war is certainly the more
> readily available.)
>> Martin Amis, Introduction to
>> *Einstein's Monsters* (1987)

> The state's duty (and it is a duty not a policy) is
> to protect the weak.

> His latest novel (*Difficulties with Girls*) features
> characters he first wrote about nearly thirty years
> ago.

When not an independent sentence (as in the
Collins example above), the bracketed information
slots into the overall structure of the existing sentence but must itself be punctuated as an independent utterance.

> When the due moment comes for her to resign
> (and who, after all, is able to judge that but her?)
> she will surely do the honourable thing.

Compare

> Forty minutes later I had claimed my cup. (There was no ceremony of presentation.) Having crammed the ebony pedestal into my kitbag, I came out into the paddock with the cup in my other hand.
>
> > Siegfried Sassoon, *Memoirs of a Fox-Hunting Man* (1928) vi.4

Occasionally there may be a question as to whether the parenthetical material should be included in brackets or placed within commas. In the example last quoted there could be no question of commas, because the parenthetical material is a complete sentence. As a rule of thumb we may say that, if the parenthesis slots into the syntactic structure of the sentence as a whole, commas should be used, since such material normally constitutes a non-defining clause:

> This painting, which probably dates from 1880 or 1881, shows all the typical features of his early manner.

From a rhetorical point of view, however, it is worth bearing in mind that brackets can be made to appear more dismissive than commas:

> He (poor fellow) could not be expected to know any better.

Another possible alternative to brackets is a dash, which is best reserved for parentheses which are casual, interjectional or have the effect of an aside:

The reason she came – and this is all entirely guesswork because she's never very forthcoming about what makes her tick – is as much a mystery as when she arrived.

An interesting particular use of round brackets is to be seen in the writing of Boswell and eighteenth-century novelists, who use it to build 'stage directions' into their narratives:

JOHNSON. 'No, Sir . . . the rest will not trouble their heads about it.' (warmly.) BOSWELL. 'Well, Sir, I cannot think so.' JOHNSON. 'Nay, Sir, there is no talking with a man who will dispute what every man knows, (angrily) don't you know this?'

James Boswell, *Life of Johnson* (1791)

(It hardly needs pointing out that in other ways too this passage exhibits now-discarded procedures of punctuation.) Compare Dickens's

'Yes; I saw what you were tending to. I hate it.'

'Hate it, Jack?' (Much bewildered.)

The Mystery of Edwin Drood (1870) ch. 2

Square brackets

These are used for wholly extraneous matter. This might arise when you wish to quote a passage which is not entirely clear as it stands (though you cannot of course alter the quotation):

> He [Verloc] came and went without any very apparent reason. He generally arrived in London (like the influenza) from the Continent, only he arrived unheralded by the Press; and his visitations set in with great severity.
>
>   Joseph Conrad, *The Secret Agent* (1907) ch. 1

The square bracket is necessary because a round one would have suggested that it was Conrad who added 'Verloc', as it does with 'like the influenza'. Square brackets are used also in scholarly contexts to offer conjectured readings in corrupt texts.

Square brackets are used by editors to supply additional information about (for example) dates, places, real names, and to give translations of foreign material:

> I think with tenderness of Dan [Benedict] sometimes, of Basil [Nigel] very rarely, of Chloe [Violet Trefusis] never. That summer [1910] I caught a heaven-sent attack of pneumonia. I arrived here yesterday [Duntreath Castle]. . . .
> *Ah Vita, je suis toute triste quand je songe combien nous ressemblons à deux joueurs* . . . . [Oh Vita, it

makes me so sad when I think how like to two
gamblers we are . . . .]
            Nigel Nicolson, *Portrait of a Marriage* (1973)

Diamond brackets

Diamond (or angle) brackets are now infrequently
seen for the same purpose. Most often they are
used to give instructions to a typist or printer.

Printers' parlance uses 'parentheses' (as does
American custom) for ( ), 'square brackets' for [ ]
and 'angle brackets' for < >.

DASHES AND DOTS

Whereas brackets are a way of holding material
together, dashes generally signify separation or
division or interruption, though the first use to be
noted resembles that of brackets.

1 *Parenthesis*

It was a matter, the whole passage – it could
only be – but of a few seconds . . .

In this sentence from Henry James's *The Wings of
the Dove* (1902, ch. 30) the use of dashes rather than

brackets gives an effect that is more emphatic, more vivid.

2   *Afterthought*

The report revealed that large numbers of young people could not identify the United Kingdom on a map of the world – a sorry reflection on our education system.

This use is possible only when the afterthought does not constitute an independent clause.

3   *Summative*

Poor spelling, a cavalier attitude to punctuation and no sense of vocabulary or sentence structure – parents might well feel a sense of despair at the education their children receive.

4   *Interruptive*

A.   As I was saying –
B.   Never mind what you were saying. Just do it.

5   *Adversative*

What's really exciting about it is – but perhaps you do not share my interest in sectional concrete?

(Under this heading come abrupt changes of subject, often accompanied by a change of sentence structure.)

6 *Preparative*

And when she got there – nothing.

Phillotson did not speak; the door was hesitatingly opened, and there entered – Sue.
Thomas Hardy, *Jude the Obscure* (1896) iv.6

This device also lends itself to comic or portentous effect; it should be used sparingly:

After all, there is but one race – humanity.
George Moore[5]

After I had resided at college seven years my father died and left me – his blessing.
Oliver Goldsmith, 'The History of the Man in Black'[6]

7 *Phatic.* A dash may be used to suggest speech which is hesitant from excitement, uncertainty, nervousness or stammering.

Get set – ready – steady – go!

I – I'm not quite sure – er – just where to start.

In older texts the dash sometimes signifies omission of all or part of a name or a piece of strong language. ('That d——d scoundrel Dr J——n!').

A dash is the only piece of punctuation (other than introductory quotes or an apostrophe as in *'tis*) that a printer will allow at the start of a line. Allowed this licence, some writers, aping continental fashion, use the dash to introduce dialogue:

> – Are you hurt, sir? Hackett asked.
>   The man politely examined each of them in turn.
> – I suppose I am, he replied.
>
> Flann O'Brien,
> *The Dalkey Archive* (1964) ch. 1

This practice, particularly with its colluding absence of other normal punctuation, is a charmless affectation.

Dots

Dots too are most often used for omission (*hiatus*), as when one doesn't want to quote the whole of a passage:

> It was the best of times, it was the worst of times . . . some of its noisiest authorities insisted on

its being received . . . in the superlative degree
of comparison only.

Charles Dickens,
A Tale of Two Cities (1859) ch. 1

They may also suggest the petering-out of an idea
or the fading-away of a voice:

There seemed little else to say . . .

If I were trying to describe London to a foreigner,
I might take Trafalgar Square and Piccadilly
Circus, the Strand and Fleet Street, the grim
wastes of Queen Victoria Street and Tottenham
Court Road, villages like Chelsea and Clapham
and Highgate struggling for individual existence,
Great Portland Street because of the secondhand
cars and the faded genial men with old school
ties, Paddington for the vicious hotels . . . and
how much would remain left out, the
Bloomsbury square with its inexpensive vice
and its homesick Indians and its sense of rainy
nostalgia, the docks . . . ?

Graham Greene,
The Lawless Roads (1939) ch. 3

Dots are used in groups of three. Where there is
a fourth dot in the row, this is the full stop – either
the first or the last, depending on where the
sentence ends.

There is a particular problem with writers – Ford
Madox Ford is one – who make frequent use of

rows of dots. How do you part-quote such a writer? A sensible solution seems to be to retain his dots and to signify editorial dots of omission by enclosing them in square brackets. Another way is to set author's dots close together and editorial dots spaced.

An account of a speech by Edmund Campion, the martyr, offers a nice instance of the mixing of dashes and dots:

> In condemning us you condemn all your own ancestors – all the ancient priests, bishops and kings . . . For what have we taught, however you may qualify it with the odious name of treason, that they did not uniformly teach? To be condemned with these lights – not of England only, but of the world – by their degenerate descendants is both gladness and glory to us.
>
> David L. Edwards, *Christian England*, vol. II: *From the Reformation to the 18th Century* (1983) p. 21

HYPHEN

The hyphen being important, and very revealing, this will be a long section for such a short mark.

The conventional wisdom is that dashes divide and hyphens join. A hyphen's work is indicated by the meaning of the word in Greek: literally 'under one', and hence 'into one' or 'together'; that is, the hyphen performs two apparently contradictory tasks. It holds together two (or more) word-elements that would not normally occur in combination (such as, well, *word-elements*, or *fish-hooks*), and keeps apart word-elements which, though linked, must be shown as separate (such as *word-elements* or *fish-hooks*).

There are three stages in the evolution of compound words: separateness (*course work*), hyphenation (*course-work*) and singleness (*coursework*). That apparently comparable words may evolve at different rates is made clear in this recent sentence: 'Millwall football club have always been *minor-league* for football but *superleague* for hooliganism'.[7] Apart from this mainly historical process, let it be noted that there are instances where the hyphen is absolutely necessary, others where there is an important distinction between the effects of hyphenation and non-hyphenation, and others again where the omission or incorrect use of hyphen causes error or ambiguity.

Fashion seems to be against the hyphen – in itself a further good reason to be for it. When we were very young we learned that if two words are yoked together to carry a single meaning the decent thing generally is to call on a hyphen – thus, *stick-in-the-mud*, *happy-go-lucky* and *man-eating tiger*. Sometimes the hyphen is not necessary, particularly if the combinations have become as fixed as, say, *court martial*, *heir apparent* or *teaspoon*. Again in general, occupations and functions can manage without (*caretaker, housemaster* and *managing direc-tor*), but *window-cleaner* can't. The character who narrates Anthony Burgess's *The Pianoplayers* (1986) insists on that form, both as meaning something different from 'pianist' and as more accurately indicating the true nature of the work involved (accompanying silent movies) than does 'piano player, with a hole between the two words'. Some latitude is possible, then, but try being free and easy (or free-and-easy) with the hyphens in *all-American boys* and *200-odd members of the Labour Party*.

As this has in recent years been a contentious area (nowhere has there been a keener clash between the niggardliness of writers and the convenience of readers), it may be prudent to start with some of the safer aspects of hyphenation, which are generally to do with incontrovertible division.

Division

1 *Syllabication*. A hyphen is used to show the syllables into which a word may be broken down, as *punc-tu-a-tion* or *A-phro-di-te*; the traditional rules were to honour etymology and to begin a syllable with a consonant, wherever possible. This sounds easy enough (though try dividing *syllable* itself), but is one of the areas where a decline in the teaching of the classical languages and the growing concern with the *look* of a page regardless of sense have done their worst damage. Moreover, it is an area where American practice differs significantly from British, notably in the world of publishing. In a recent letter in the *Sunday Times*[8] an author (British) reported the tribulations of having her work typeset in the United States, which resulted in divisions such as *chil-dren*, *youn-ger* and *psychol-ogy*. It is therefore fitting that it should have been the United States that gave us the message that 'Breaking up is hard to do'. British practice is not beyond reproach, either, as these examples make clear:

> . . . row upon row of Victorian housing, limited and uni-maginative, now being swept away . . . .

> Of course Catholics were – not always wrongly – accused of wishing for foreign (Spanish) dominance. And some of t-he arguments in Fawkes's favour might equally be used in palliation of the Pro-visional IRA's murderous tactics.

> Townsend's simple goal on the hour, courtesy of a mish-eader by Liverpool's captain . . . .[9]

2 *Hesitation*. Stammering, sobbing, gasping, dithering or speaking slowly-as-to-an-idiot-child-or-foreigner is often represented by hyphens:

I Clau-Clau-Clau-Claudius

Once, at a wedding-breakfast, the woman at my side inquired of the three-year-old boy opposite as he struggled with his cutlery, 'Are-you-am-bi-dex-trous?'

> The Father desperate with jealousy, stuttering in anger – 'No n-notice. N-no notice. God damn it, the mean old bugger.'
>
> Beryl Bainbridge, *A Quiet Life* (1976) ch. 2

A related use is to signify laughter, as in this example from Hardy's *Tess of the d'Urbervilles:*

> 'Ho-ho-ho!' laughed dark Cat.
> 'Hee-hee-hee!' laughed the tippling bride. . . .
> 'Heu-heu-heu!' laughed dark Cat's mother.

3 *Incompletion*. If a word is left incomplete at the end of a line, a hyphen is inserted to indicate the fact; the cautions as to sense and etymology noted above apply equally here. The hyphen goes at the end, never the start, of a line, and what precedes the hyphen must be sensible (*argu-ing*, not *ar-guing* or *arg-uing*).

4 *Suspension*. Indicated here is what Partridge ringingly calls the 'deferent or suspensive or annunciatory hyphen'.[10] Briefly, this means that if a sentence has a number of hyphenated elements, but with some words omitted to avoid tedious repetition, the appropriate hyphens must be retained to preserve the sense of the sentence:

> It is the utmost folly to expect a two- or three- or even four-year-old to handle cutlery with skill.

If this sometimes means that accuracy is to be bought at the price of awkwardness, re-cast the sentence and do the job properly.

5 *Quotation.* When an element is quoted separately from the word to which it belongs, a hyphen may be used before the element, or after it, or both:

> In *telescope, tele-* refers to distance, and *-scope* to looking.

> In *prestidigitation, -digi-* indicates the fingers.

Combination

The second main function of hyphenation, which could be discussed, argued over and illustrated at all but infinite length, is that of forming compounds or combinations of words. This is the really contentious stuff.

In *The King's English* (3rd edn, 1930), the Fowlers, not normally a by-word for the kind of typographic permissiveness current fifty years after they were writing, decreed that the hyphen should be dropped wherever reason permitted. No argument there, brothers. Where the arguments start is over what is reasonable.

Again, let's begin with the easy stuff. A hyphen is what you need to avoid glaring ambiguity: three farthing candles (which probably means nothing anyway to people born after the 1940s) means nothing at all without a well-placed hyphen; *four minute eggs* could mean either of two things.

Related to this is the use of hyphens in compound words of which the constituent elements have forsaken their separate meanings: *forget-me-not*, *love-in-a-mist* and (from darts, I suppose) *three-in-a-bed*.

Partridge, with daunting thoroughness, discusses possible hyphenations under seven major headings and more than a hundred minor ones. The reader looking for such a comprehensive treatment is recommended to the relevant pages of *You Have a Point There*, though with the caution that since the book appeared (1953) there have been significant changes in attitudes to punctuation generally and especially to hyphenation. In particular, with something like what Partridge calls 'the speeding up [hyphen needed there?] of modern life', Americans have charged ahead with the suppression of the hyphen.[11] He adds that if we find some of their innovations initially off-putting (*offputting?*), we shall nevertheless eventually find them guilty of nothing worse than 'intelligent anticipation'. It is certainly true that there is now a strong tendency towards minimal hyphenation, often at the expense of clarity (whether by making solids – *rewrite* for *re-write* – or by unstringing the beads: *end of course module test*). The following guidelines acknowledge the inevitability of the change, and the desirability of some of it, but identify instances where there can be no alternative to hyphenation (and *Hart* gives long lists of words now recognised as dispensing with a hyphen).

1 *To prevent ambiguity.* Hyphens are needed when similar words have different meanings: *represent, re-present; reform, re-form; recover, re-cover, remark, re-mark.* (Compare the slightly, but crucially, different *correspondent* and *co-respondent.* The *Independent* for 14 January 1989 captioned a photograph 'Freddie Garrity, 51-year-old singer of reformed Sixties pop group Freddie and the Dreamers'). When a number of words are grouped together a hyphen shows which are to be understood as going together: *an Irish linen-manufacturer, an Irish-linen manufacturer; a French letter-machine, a French-letter machine; a pickled-herring magnate, a pickled herring-magnate.*

2 *With numbers.* Compound cardinal numbers (*thirty-seven, forty-two*) need hyphens, as do their corresponding ordinals (*his thirty-seventh appearance for England*). *Five hundred* and *ten thousand* do without, but *five-hundredth anniversary* and *ten-thousandth customer* do not. Fractions when they are compounds take a hyphen (*two-fifths of her time, five-eighths of a pound*), but not when they indicate separate items (*three quarters of the men wore dinner jackets, and the other quarter lounge suits*). Hyphens are needed also when dealing with dates as they are given in Amis's *Difficulties with Girls*: 'contract signed one-eight-sixty-four, for delivery one-one-sixty-six, 500 advanced, delivered twenty-twelve-sixty-five'.

The greatest difficulty with hyphens is over compounds, which are discussed below according to type.

Any compound noun which has grown to be regarded uncontroversially as a single word and which has only one stress requires no hyphen (*dustman, newspaper*). Most compounds of all kinds with more than one stress need a hyphen (*cross-question, argy-bargy, long-term*).

3 *Noun and noun.* Generally no problems here: *Wigan–London train, man–woman interaction.** When

---

* In printed texts, as here, it is normal to use a short, unspaced dash instead of a hyphen to join elements that are linked but separate (that is, where the dash could be replaced by 'and' or 'to'). This is not an option available on a typewriter. Any potential difficulty with this sort of material may be avoided by substituting a virgule for the hyphen or dash, as

the elements are themselves hyphenated, higher
canons of style must prevail; for example: no
writer who could even consider 'fly-by-night-go-
between', should be allowed a pen. *Age-group*,
blood-group and, relative newcomer, *peer-group*, are
all better for a hyphen. *God–King*, *player–coach* are
much the same as posh names such as *Dyer-Ball*
and *Steele-Bodger*. Britons like *man-power* and *horse-
power*, but Americans do not, and British practice
is anyway changing under the pressure for *-person*
or *person* combinations. Do scientists still use things
like *foot-pounds*? Three-in-a-beds need hyphens:
wear-and-tear, *rack-and-ruin*. Even those who argue
for no hyphen in *T-square* and *X-ray* and *U-boat*
have to concede it when these are used adjectivally.
Almost anything that re-duplicates needs a
hyphen: *bang-bang*, *topsy-turvy*, *slap-dash*, *tick-tock*.
As noted, many familiar compounds to do with
occupations have become solids, but newer ones
(*computer-programmer*) and some old ones (*bee-
keeper*, *mischief-maker*) haven't. Where the first element is in the possessive case (often so with plants
and flowers), the hyphen is generally unavoidable
(*Juno's-tongue*, *Joseph's-coat*), but there are exceptions (*coltsfoot*, *wolfsbane*).

---

in *Wigan/London train*, or *man/woman interaction*. The advantages
are more apparent when there is a longer series of items,
especially if one of them has more than one element:
California/Mid-West/New England is clearly preferable to any
possible alternative using hyphens. (The virgule is also often
found as a shorthand for 'or': *and/or* is itself a case in point.)

4 *Noun and adjective.* It largely depends which order the adjective and noun come in. Adjective–noun compounds generally do not require hyphenation (*corrugated iron, First Secretary, fifteenth century, national coach*). Noun–adjective compounds have until comparatively recently been slower to discard the hyphen, but the trend is now accelerating, and we shall soon be left only with such die-hard cases as *attorney-general* and (at a pinch) *sum-total*. Either way it should go without saying that where compounds of either group are used attributively (i.e. as adjectives) there is no question of omitting the hyphen: *corrugated-iron roofs, a poverty-stricken family, a blood-red sunset*; and compare *ice-cold, large-scale, stage-struck*. An adverb or adjective preceding such a combination does not normally require hyphenation (*a late fifteenth-century manuscript*); *mid-* is the exception (*a mid-fifteenth-century manuscript*). The hyphen can also be used with telling effect, often ironically, as was shown in a *Times Literary Supplement* letter in 1987 that referred to a 'putting-him-in-his-place review'. In the summer and autumn of 1988 there were frequent spoken descriptions of Ronald Reagan as (presumably in this form) 'the about-to-be-ex-President of the United States'.

5 *Adverb compounds.* As a rule, when an adverb modifies an adjective no hyphen is needed (*a tastefully renovated house, a beautifully bound book, a stupidly untypical cruelty*). The exception comes in cases where the first element might not be instantly recognised as an adverb – *old, well, new* (*an old-fashioned notion, a well-known broadcaster, a new-fangled tango*). When such combinations are used predicatively (i.e. after a verb) no hyphen is required since no risk of misunderstanding exists: *excessive public mourning is old fashioned, his foibles are well known. Half* is an odd case on which there is not always agreement. Even predicatively, *half-hearted* is better hyphenated (*his effort was half-hearted*). *Half a dozen, half an hour* and *half a pound* might go either way, but the forms *a half-dozen, a half-hour* and *a half-pound* are mandatory. *I half expected this* is all right unless there is a strong feeling that the words form a single idea, as in *I half-opened the packet*. A hyphen is optional but (regrettably) disappearing in *half-way, half-past (two)*; mandatory in *half-day, half-holiday, half-hearted, half-pay, half-price, half-term, half-time, half-truth, half-wit(ted), half-yearly*. (When in doubt with *half*, hyphenate – you won't often be seriously wrong.)

Adverb–participle combinations are hyphenated, whether attributive or predicative (*a new-born child is a joy, I like my eggs hard-boiled*). The preferred English way of ruining good beef is to have it *well-done*.

When the adverb comes second the hyphen is indispensable: *lay-by, get-out, go-ahead, stand-in*.

6 *-ed*. Compound adjectives on the model *adjective/noun + noun + -ed* must be hyphenated: *a man-sized tissue, a back-handed compliment*.

7   *Prefixes*. Several points to note here.

A hyphen is always needed when attaching a prefix to a noun or adjective that takes a capital letter: *un-English, pro-Axis, anti-Russian, crypto-Thatcherite*.

Though the practice is becoming less general, many compounds have been formed by using a hyphen to attach a prefix to a noun. For example, *by-, ex-,* non-, ante-, anti-, pro-, re-* and *sub-* have been combined with nouns to give *by-pass, non-aggression, ante-natal, anti-smoking, re-do* and *sub-let*. Although abundance of instances is now giving an air of familiarity to items such as *nonresistance, prewar* and *reintegrate* that only very recently were odd-looking, a number of cautions are in order. First, the hyphen should be (often isn't, but *should* be) retained where its omission causes a doubling-up of letters: *cooperate, reemploy, misshapen*. It is not really an answer to say that where vowels are involved you can get round the problem by using a diaeresis (*coöperate*). This has never looked at home in English, and if you are going to that amount of trouble you might as well use the hyphen in the first place. Secondly, an imposed break at the end of a line can make bad worse, as in this from the *Guardian*: 'and so once again a World Cup began with scrappy disco-

---

* Care needed with *ex-*. The young woman who talked of having married her 'ex-English teacher' was surprised to be asked how he enjoyed being now Belgian or Slovenian or whatever it was he had become.

ordinated football'. Discussing this example, Wood observes that two hyphens would be ugly (*dis-co-ordinated*), so 'the only alternative is to duplicate letters and write *dis-coordinated*'. Surely not! *Unco-ordinated*? The best alternative is to scrap the whole thing and start the sentence again without such an ugly word. And what are we to do with the newcomer *co-coordinator*? Thirdly, prefixes with *re-* need careful handling for three reasons: (1) there is a difference of meaning between *reassure* and *re-assure*; (2) the hyphen *must* be retained if there is a strong sense of doing over again (with effort or difficulty, perhaps) – *re-write* as against *rewrite*; (3) although we are becoming used to *re-* words written as solids, they do still, in this interim period, appear odd (*redo*), particularly when vowels are conspicuous (*reirrigate*, *reuse*, *reopt*). In no other area of their work do writers so revealingly indicate their tact and sensitivity to the reader.

What the last examples stress is the truth that the hyphen is, as Fowler puts it, not 'an ornament but an aid to understanding'. How crass therefore are the institutions and publications which drop the hyphen, whenever remotely possible, in the interests of design or house style. The result is *coauthorship*, *coattails* and *preempt*. *De gustibus* and all that, but these words look unnatural to me, and seem to require a reader-aloud to make some peculiar noises, as do *loophole* and *chophouse*.

Without hyphens a line may be easier to justify, but the resulting loss of easy intelligibility certainly isn't.

Some writers take great care with hyphens. Graham Greene at times adheres to conventions which are now outmoded (as with *Oxford-street*), and others go to the opposite extreme (as with *ashheap*); sometimes he just gets it wrong, as in *The Comedians*, where he uses *Negro-successor* (or someone who succeeds Negroes) when he obviously means a successor who is a Negro. Kingsley Amis, at least in his early novels, has *to-day* and *to-morrow*, as Thomas Hardy had *to-year*. Such scrupulousness may seem over-cautious, but is greatly preferable to the indifference (i.e. discourtesy to the reader) manifested in *coworker* and *deice* and to the illiteracy of *superfluous hair-remover*.

These reflections, never far away when reading nowadays, were brought to mind by a recent re-appearance (*sic*) of the 'fine tooth-comb' problem. The problem is the misapprehension that this seems to suggest a dentist's instrument of torture, despite the *OED*'s sanction: 'a small-tooth comb', on the model of *tooth-rail* rather than *tooth-glass* – that is, composed of rather than made for. Horsy folk use the 'fine-tooth comb' for the same purpose as (some may think) writers of books on punctuation, i.e. nit-picking. That the issues are not so marginal, however, may be emphasised by a final example. The words *extra marital sex* may or may not indicate something good, but they certainly indicate something different according to the use or non-use of a hyphen. In this respect, readers may wish to consider the punctuation of the following items: *five inch long strips, twenty three ton lorries; loud speaker; well built* (man or woman); *a cross section of the orchestra.* Joyce in *Ulysses* (1922) uses many non-hyphenated words which still have a strange look to them more than half-a-century later: *Inkeraser, saucestains, hoofthuds, halffed.* The use of hyphens with repeated letters can be used to give a variety of effects, as in these examples from Browning and Thackeray:

> And I've lost you, lost myself,
> Lost all-l-l-l-
>> Browning,
> *Men and Women* (1855)

What a beautiful, *byoo-ootiful* song that was you sang last night.
>> Thackeray, *Vanity Fair* (1848) ch. 4

Hyphens are not needed with such things as *B flat* and *C flat minor*, even when these are used adjectivally; note *folk-song* (but *folk music*), and there is no hyphen in *Vaughan Williams*.

INVERTED COMMAS

Alternative names are 'punctuation marks', 'speech marks', 'quotation marks'. All of these are rather a mouthful, and none accurately covers all the purposes to which the marks are put. It would now perhaps be best to adopt *quotes*, which has been growing in colloquial frequency lately, in the probably vain hope of restricting it to that and leaving *quotations* alone as *quotations*.

What appears in quotes is to be understood as either words actually spoken or direct quotations from a printed source.

Direct speech

> *There was spoken dialogue appearing between quotation marks.*
>
> **Kingsley Amis,** *One Fat Englishman*
> (1963) ch. 7

Only words actually spoken are to be enclosed in quotes:

> 'Yes,' said Valentine.
> 'I expect my sister told you,' said Aunt Irene.
> 'Yes,' said Valentine.
>
> **Alice Thomas Ellis,** *The 27th Kingdom*
> (1982) ch. 2

Compare *Aunt Irene said she expected her sister had told him.*

Yes, Mr Bhoolaboy had said, the sacked *mali*'s tools could be made available. He could even suggest a boy, able, willing, if not very bright.

Paul Scott, *Staying On* (1978)

The rules for the positioning of full stops in relation to inverted commas are quite straightforward.

If a sentence begins and ends with words actually spoken, the full stop goes inside the final inverted commas. This is true of both the following kinds of sentence:

'I cannot be sure but I think the woman has been lying.'

'I cannot be sure,' said Sir Ralph, 'but I think the woman has been lying.'

The logic of this is that inverted commas go before and after what has been said. If what has been said is a sentence, it ends with a full stop. Therefore the final full inverted commas must include, must follow the full stop (or final full stop if there is more than one):

'It is a wicked world,' said Sir Ralph, 'in which bimbos can ruin a man's reputation. These kiss'n'tell types are no more than slags with a press agent.'

For the same reasons, any other relevant punctuation belonging to the sentence spoken is placed inside the inverted commas:

'You clumsy boy!' the fat woman shouted. 'Why cannot you ride your bicycle on the pavement?'

It should in fairness be pointed out that an alternative system deals differently with quoted material that is itself a sentence, thus:

She sighed to herself, 'I wish he were here.'

Logically two full stops are required here, one inside and one outside the quotes, and it may seem more sensible to elide the earlier one, placing the full stop after the quotes. In that case, however, it might seem that the quoted sentence was incomplete, and thus the above version is almost universally preferred in print. (In America the practice in such circumstances is to place the full stop inside the quotes, regardless of whether the utterance is complete. This used also to be the case in Britain, but modern practice is more discriminatory.)

Notice the difference between

I yelled out, 'Give me your hand!'

and

How sadly few are those who can truthfully claim, 'I did my best'!

Note also

'What exactly does it mean,' she said, 'to be a "feminist"?'

Where an element of *he said / she said* intervenes in a sentence, that element is marked off with commas, as in the sentences given above, i.e.:

'. . . . . ,' he said, '. . . . .'

Where that element occurs at the end of a sentence, the punctuation is as follows:

'Yes, of course, if it's fine tomorrow,' said Mrs Ramsay.
'But you'll have to be up with the lark,' she added.

Virginia Woolf, *To the Lighthouse* (1927) ch. 1

An older school of writers introduced direct speech with a colon, as in these examples from Graham Greene's *A Gun for Sale* (1936) and Anthony Powell's *A Question of Upbringing* (1951):

Sir Marcus said venomously: 'You're a fool, Davis. If he's going to kill us anyway –'

Templer said: 'It is much more like Le Bas.'

Note also the arrangement here:

Mr Bhoolaboy said, 'The sacked *mali*'s tools can be made available to him'.[12]

Increasingly the fashion is for single inverted commas ('   ') rather than double ("   "), though these are still preferred by, for example, *Times* publications. The important thing is to be consistent, though the use of single quotes does have disadvantages, particularly when the last word quoted is a genitive:

'The style of this is unmistakably Tess's.'

'If it's Amis's,' he said, 'it will sell at least as well as Burgess's.'

This kind of thing makes the reader's life unnecessarily more difficult.

Adopting the modern convention (as Macmillan publications do), we can say that where something is quoted within words actually spoken that quotation should be given in double quotes:

'John Clayton,' he remembered, 'was always

fond of those lines "What is this life, if, full of care . . .".'

'Did you hear the accused say "It's a fair cop, guv" or not?' asked counsel for the prosecution.

Talking of his notes on Shakespeare, he said, 'I despise those who do not see that I am right in the passage where *as* is repeated, and "asses of great charge" introduced. That on "To be, or not to be," is indisputable.'

James Boswell, *Life of Johnson* (1791), May 1776

'I am Aunt Irene,' Aunt Irene told the girl who stood before her in the hallway. 'Pronounced "Irene" to rhyme with "serener", rather than "Irene" to rhyme with "insane", or "Irene" to rhyme with "teeny weeny", or "Irene" to rhyme with "unseen".'

Alice Thomas Ellis, *The 27th Kingdom*
(1982) ch. 2

(Material within the double quotes is given within single quotes again.)

Material within the double quotes is subject to the normal rules of punctuation, as is the larger sentence of which it is a part. There can be difficulties with novels which employ first-person narrators who report the remarks of others. Conrad's work offers particular examples:

'I started the lame engine ahead. "It must be this miserable trader – this intruder," exclaimed the manager, looking back malevolently at the place we had left. "He must be English," I said.

' "It will not save him from getting into trouble if he is not careful," muttered the manager darkly.'

Heart of Darkness (1902)

Occasionally (better: rarely) quotes may be used to suggest irony or scepticism:

although of course the Ufford . . . would fall into disfavour from time to time, usually on account of some 'incivility' offered him by the management or staff

Anthony Powell, *The Acceptance World* (1955)

his 'work' now connected with some charitable organisation

ibid.

he cut them off in midsentence with, 'Ah, you're speaking in inverted commas', thus suggesting that they couldn't be serious, could they?

John Mortimer, 'Robinson's Law',
Listener, 28 July 1988

The convention with direct speech has been to start a fresh line for each new speech. How (as they say) 'user-friendly' that convention is was highlighted by Malcolm Bradbury's *The History Man* (very modern), which dispensed with it and was far less readable in consequence.

Quotation

Quotations naturally go inside quotes, but not always. Those which have passed into common usage, whether as idioms or as clichés, require no marks: *comparisons are odorous; The lady doth protest too much, methinks; foregone conclusion; it is a far, far better thing that I do.* Quotations of some length, whether in verse or prose, may be introduced by a colon and set out as a separate chunk of print; no quotes are required in this case (unless, of course, they occur within the quoted passages). If long prose material is not set out in this way, the introductory quotes must be repeated at the beginning of each successive paragraph (not of every line as in olden days) as well as at the end of the passage. Where short quotations are incorporated within the structure of a sentence they must be marked:

Even people who know no Shakespeare have heard 'To be or not to be'.

A special case of quotation is that of proverbs, saws and other received wisdom. These require no quotes if being said routinely, but quotes help if a particular point is being made: 'lips that touch kippers shall never touch mine'.

A final cautionary note. A sad demonstration of the truth that punctuation is for the page and not for performance came with the resignation in November 1988 of Herr Philipp Jenninger, president of the West German Bundestag. In a speech that attempted to explain why Germans had supported Hitler and later suppressed their memories and guilt, he appeared to his outraged audience to be justifying these things. As the *Independent* (2 November 1988) put it, 'To listeners who could not know that in the written text the expressions *"Lebensraum"*, "Jewish *Untermenschen"* and "vermin" appeared in quotation marks, it sounded as though Mr Jenninger was blithely appropriating Nazi terminology'.

Names and titles

Hand-written scripts should use quotes (or underlining; the print equivalent is italics) for names of trains and boats and planes: *Stephenson's 'Rocket'*, *the 'QE2'* (not *'the QE2'*). Similarly in names of newspapers and journals initial *The* is not included in quotes: *the 'Listener'*, *the 'Spectator'*, *the 'Guardian'*. (For no clear reason *'The Times'* and *'The Economist'* are often treated as exceptions to this practice; but compare *the 'Times' leader*, where the article relates to *leader* and not *Times*.) Note also that italic or underlining is not used for the possessive in 'the *Guardian*'s new lay-out' (with quotes this is a problem). It is an illiteracy to use quotes for the names of houses, inns and hotels, as it is to use them with the heading of a notice which is made prominent by other graphic means such as capitalisation, underlining or colour. Titles of books and plays should appear in quotes or be underlined: *Carry On, Jeeves!*, *Much Ado about Nothing*, *Lyrical Ballads*. The advantage in handwriting of underlining titles is that it leaves quotes free for identifying individual elements within a larger work:

This week's *Listener* has an article called 'Where the bee sucks'.

His *Kingsley Amis: An English Moralist* has a chapter called 'Kingsley and the Women'.

'Tintern Abbey' was first printed in *Lyrical Ballads*.

Other things being equal, titles of short poems are given in quotes ('Daffodils', 'Porphyria's Lover'), whilst longer ones have their titles underlined or italicised (*The Ancient Mariner*, *The Wreck of the 'Deutschland'*, *Paradise Lost*). As a rule, initial *The* in literary titles should be underlined or italicised ('Coleridge's *The Ancient Mariner*').

It is also handy, of course, to see the distinction between Macbeth and *Macbeth*, Emma and *Emma*, and so on.

Hymns and poems generally known and referred to by their first line should be given in quotes: 'I wandered lonely as a cloud'. Current practice is to omit quotes and italics in referring to the Bible and its books (note – no capital in *biblical*), as it is with the religious writings of other faiths (the Koran, the Vedas). Where a work is familiarly known by the name of a person traditionally associated with it (Wisden, Bradshaw, Old Moore, Brewer, Fowler, Roget), that name has not conventionally been given quotes, italics or underlining, but there seems no reason why it should not, being now equivalent to a title. Other standard reference works have quotes/italics/underlining as standard (*OED*, *DNB*, Gray's *Anatomy*).

Though this is not, strictly speaking, a matter for quotes alone, this is an appropriate place to identify some of the procedures to be used in writing references to printed sources. It is not possible to offer guidelines that will be universally applicable, since publishing-houses and journals have different preferences and requirements in this respect; for example, most publishers now prefer single quotes, but *Times* publications still use double. However, there is a large body of agreement, and the guidelines offered below will help those preparing a hand- or type-written text. Whatever the medium ultimately envisaged – script, type or print – the main thing is to be consistent.

References to books are normally given as (for example)

David Crystal, *The English Language* (Harmondsworth, 1988), p. 100

or

Baines, C. P., *A Topical History of Billinge* (London, 1964), vol. ii, p. 100.

A contemporary tendency is to slim down the references by omitting 'vol.' and 'p.', thus:

Baines, C. P., *A Topical History of Billinge*, ii, 100.

Titles (and details of place and year of publication) need not be given in full after the first reference, provided a clear short title is indicated for subsequent citations. Articles in periodicals and chapters in books should be given in quotes (and printed in roman type), with the title of the periodical or book underlined or in italics:

'Cecilia Strickland (1741–1814)', *North West Catholic History*, vol. xv (1988), pp. 1–5.

In scientific works, titles of papers are printed without quotes. Houses differ about conventions for page numbers, but a safe guide is to use the fewest possible figures consistent with clarity. The Macmillan guidance to authors gives as examples: *32–3, 132–48, 200–5*; the exception is 'teen' numbers, where the *1* is repeated: *1914–18*.

Just as *period* and *full stop* have become words that people say and write, as well as marks they make on paper, so *quote* too has become a word people speak, often accompanying it with a silly waggle of the fingers; this device normally indicates scepticism or disdain, or betrays a speaker too lazy to look for the right word for the occasion.

As at the end of Chapter 2, some quotations are given from recent writers illustrating the use(s) or non-use of the marks described above.

Rightho . . . Roughish . . . .

Evelyn Waugh,
Officers and Gentlemen (1955) ch. 1

Readers of the upmarket daily papers
Independent, 6 July 1988

. . . a Moorish-Tudor-God-knows-what-of-a-lamp . . . .

Graham Greene,
Brighton Rock (1930) vii. 7

Their eyes gave out an eager-spirited light that resembled near-genius . . . . sometimes a lavatory chain would dangle over nothing from a fourth- or fifth-floor ceiling . . . . she was so well built, fair and healthy looking.

Muriel Spark, *The Girls of Slender Means* (1963) chs 1, 2

Webster's was not an off-the-top-of-the-head performance.

Whitney F. Bolton, *A Living Language* (Princeton, NJ, 1982) p.413

. . . it [a writer's style] varies according to whether he is writing for himself, or for his friends, his teachers or his God, for an educated upper class, a waiting-to-be-educated lower class or a hostile jury. . . . Style then is the relation between what a writer wants to say; his subject – and himself – or the powers which he has: between the form of his subject and the content of his parts.

Cyril Connolly, *Enemies of Promise* (1938) ch. 2

'And that's so rare these days, isn't it? – with all this running off and divorcing and all the . . . Oh, I'm sorry, Roger, how terrible tactless of me. I didn't mean –'

'That's perfectly all right, Grace.'

'I do feel so –'

'Say no more.' Or else stand by for a dose of bodily harm (Roger thought to himself),

you women's - cultural - lunch - club - organising
Saturday Review of Literature-reading substantial-
inheritance-from-soft-drink-corporation-awaiting
old-New-Hampshire-family-invoking Kennedy-
loving just-wunnerful-labelling Yank bag.

Kingsley Amis,
One Fat Englishman (1963) ch. 2

'My boy has been injured in the foot,' said
Lady Circumference coldly.

'Dear me! Not badly, I hope? Did he twist his
ankle in the jumping?'

'No,' said Lady Circumference, 'he was shot
at by one of the assistant masters. But it is kind
of you to inquire.'

'Three Miles Open!' announced Paul. 'The
course of six laps will be run as before.'

Evelyn Waugh, *Decline and Fall* (1928) ch. 8.

' "You knew him best," I repeated. And perhaps she did. But with every word spoken
the room was growing darker, and only her
forehead, smooth and white, remained illumined
by the unextinguishable light of belief and love.

' "You were his friend," she went on. "His
friend," she repeated, a little louder. "You must
have been, if he had given you this, and sent
you to me. I feel I can speak to you – and oh! I
must speak. I want you – you who have heard
his last words – to know I have been worthy of
him . . . It is not pride . . . Yes! I am proud to

know I understood him better than any one on earth – he told me so himself. And since his mother died I have had no one – no one – to – to –"

'I listened [. . .].'

Joseph Conrad, Heart of Darkness (1902)

'We shall miss you, Jasper, at the "Alternate Musical Wednesdays" to-night; but no doubt you are best at home. Good night. God bless you! "Tell me, shep-herds, te-e-ell me; tell me-e-e, have you seen (have you seen, have you seen, have you seen) my-y-y Flo-o-ora pass this way!"' melodiously good Minor Canon the Reverend Septimus Crisparkle thus delivers himself, in musical rhythm, as he withdraws his amiable face from the doorway and conveys it downstairs.

Charles Dickens, The Mystery of
Edwin Drood (1870) ch. 2

. . . such is human nature, and young-lady-nature especially.

Anthony Trollope, The Warden (1855) ch. 7

'Mickey's doing research at the Courtauld; that's why we're here.'
'Oh really?' (Oh Christ) 'What into?'

Julian Barnes, Metroland (1980) ii.3

Or would 'adult' be a better word, a more . . . 'adult' word?

Ibid., iii

4

Writer/Printer/Reader

Of all the subjects which engage the attention of the compositor none proves a greater stumbling-block or is so much a matter of uncertainty and doubt, especially to the mere tyro, as the Art of Punctuation. This arises partly from the necessarily somewhat inexact nature of the art itself, but far more from ignorance of the principles on which its rules ought to be founded, and the illogical construction of the sentences with which the printer sometimes has to deal.

Henry Beadnell,
Spelling and Punctuation (1880)

At the end of Chapter 3, attention was drawn to one of the differences between hand-writing and printing, i.e. the convention of underlining the titles of books (or putting them in quotes) when a printed text will italicise them. In a number of respects, different systems have to be followed in written and in printed texts. This chapter briefly identifies some features of the presentation of a text that are (virtually) exclusive to print, many of them having to do with emphasis.

CAPITAL LETTERS

'Why, here's a J,' said Joe, 'and a O equal to anythink! Here's a J and a O, Pip, and a J-O, Joe.'
Charles Dickens, *Great Expectations* (1861) ch. 7

Capital is derived ultimately from the stem *capit-* of *caput* (Latin for 'head'). In writing, a capital letter is distinguished by greater height, and in printing sometimes by a different form also; small capitals (see below) have the form of capitals but the height of small letters. Vallins offers a useful caution on their use:

Outside fairly well-defined limits, the writer has to walk warily in a kind of no-man's-land . . . the good writer will observe the main conventions; but beyond these he has the privilege and responsibility of deciding between . . . capitals and small letters. His use of capitals, like his punctuation generally, should exactly correspond with his meaning.[1]

The well-defined limits are easily stated and probably widely known, even today. A capital letter starts the first word in a sentence. Its other principal uses are with proper nouns.

In sentences

This sentence begins with a capital letter.

Similarly with 'internal' sentences, a capital will follow such devices as a question mark, a dash or a colon:

The stall-holder replied, 'You picked the fruit yourself, so you cannot complain.'

If only part of the sentence is quoted, the quotation has no capital:

It was described as having had 'one careful owner'.

A complete sentence within brackets should start with a capital, but if it is bracketed within another sentence then no capital should be used. Compare

A certain snobbery attaches to literary kinds, even today. (The value of any judgement on social grounds is, of course, very moot.) One even meets readers who perversely delight in endorsing demotic forms over higher ones.

Number 17, Gough Square has a large garret (the word is defined in Johnson's Dictionary as 'a room on the highest floor of the house') which occupies the whole length and breadth of the building. . . .

John Wain, *Samuel Johnson* (1974) ch. 9

A sentence following a dash always starts with a small letter, as, ideally, should one following a colon:

The amount of coursework required is excessive: it will have to be reduced.

She is a game little fighter – there's no chance at all of her giving in.

In words

Three words conventionally take a capital. These are the vocative *O* and the exclamatory *Oh* (see p. 69). The nominative of the first-person pronoun (*I*) is the only one to take a capital. An occasional exception is *He* when applied to God, but not always to Jesus, and other exceptions are *Who* and *His/Him* when referring to God; it is quite common nowadays for writers, whether for theological or punctuational reasons, not to use capitals in this case. Compare this exchange between a believer and non-believer in Graham Greene's *A Burnt-Out Case* (1961):

> 'Of course, but if it hadn't been His will . . .'
> 'Perhaps it's his will that you should take a nembutal.'

The first-person pronoun (*I*) was not capitalised in early forms of English (*ic*, *ich*) and no other Indo-European language distinguishes it in this way. The capitalisation was introduced by early printers to avoid confusion with variant forms such as *i*, *j* and the *I* which was a specialised use of 'long I' to represent 'ego'. Abstractions generally do (or *can*) take capitals, particularly in literary contexts:

> She sat like Patience on a monument
> Shakespeare, *Twelfth Night*, II.iv.111

> Faith, Hope and Charity

Notwithstanding the mileage Shakespeare gets out of punning on *Will* in Sonnets 135 and 143, it is prudent when dabbling with the law to use *Will* to signify one's last will and testament. Some trademarks and brand-names have become generic for the objects they are attached to: *hoover*, *instamatic*, *durex*, *sellotape* and *xerox*. These require no capital for ordinary purposes; otherwise brand names are a set of proper nouns and should be capitalised accordingly: *Hotpoint, Cadillac, Sanyo.*

Literary uses

Lines of verse, whether in poetry or in song, used to be set out with a capital at the start of each line regardless of syntax:

> Sigh no more, ladies, sigh no more,
>   Men were deceivers ever;
> One foot in sea, and one on shore,
>   To one thing constant never.
>   Shakespeare, *Much Ado*
>   *about Nothing*, ii.iii.60–3

A modern tendency, arguing (perhaps, or perhaps not) that the division into lines is itself sufficient guidance to the reader, is to print verse as prose. (Whether this tendency is or is not characterised also by a tendency to *write* verse as if it were prose is a question outside our present scope.) In giving references to texts, the tradition of heavy punctuation makes full use of capitals:

In *The Logic and the Epistemological Sanctions of Dr Johnson's Arguments*, Volume i, Part i, Chapter 2, she refers to Augustine's *Summa Theologiae*, Volume xi, pp. 9–11.

When a reference is less complex than this one, small letters will often suffice (e.g. Williams, *Descartes*, ch. 5). Letters in an epistolary sense may be considered here: not just *Dear* . . . to start but *Yours* (capital) *faithfully* or *sincerely* (no capital); other signings-off should be capitalised on at least the first word (*Love, With best wishes, Cheers*). In highly formal signings-off (as in writing to a pope or cardinal) every part of the addressee's title should be capitalised:

> I have the honour to be, my Lord Cardinal, Your Eminence's devoted and most obedient child . . . .

Proper nouns

Lots of categories here. A capital letter is required for the names of people and places, including important buildings and large geographical features (*William Shakespeare, England, St Paul's Cathedral, the Thames*); for titles of trains and boats and planes, regiments, newspapers, days and saints' days (see p. 47) and days of national or other importance (*Christmas Day, Labour Day, VJ Day*), but the seasons are generally uncapitalised; for titles (*Queen Elizabeth, Pope John Paul*, but 'in English history relations between queen and pope have not always been amicable'; *President Lincoln, the Emperor Nero*; for races, nations, peoples, tribes and the languages they speak; for derivatives of proper nouns (Augustan literature, Leavisite criticism, Wagnerian noise). A common noun, if individualised, becomes in effect a proper noun: *I shall have to ask Mummy, His Holiness is expecting me*. Nicknames and pet names likewise: 'Get a move on, Smudger!'

Names and titles made up of several words generally use capitals throughout, except for articles and prepositions (*the Department of Trade and Industry, the British Library*); an exception is *The Hague* (compare *the Netherlands*). As we have seen, some newspapers insist on capitalised *The* as part of their title. On subsequent references the capital may be (and nowadays usually is) dropped: *De La Salle College – the College* or *college; the Great War – the war; the Royal Academy – the academy*. This growing convention should not apply in specialised cases where there is the possibility of misunderstanding: *the House of Commons – the House; Hampstead Heath – the Heath; Scotland Yard – the Yard*. Titles and terms of address are capitalised: *Her Majesty the Queen, His Royal Highness, Your Holiness, Your Worship*.

Capitals are also used for abbreviations formed from initials: *OED, ASH, ID, VCR*. Sometimes writers, particularly journalists, will in the interests of space give the full name on its first occurrence only, indicating in brackets the abbreviation to be used thereafter. Alternatively, if the abbreviation is to be used throughout with only a slight risk of the reader's not being familiar with it, the practice is to explain it on its first occurrence: *ASH (Action* *on Smoking and Health*). If there is a strong possibility that the reader may be unfamiliar with the topic it is good manners as well as good sense to explain the item as well as the abbreviation: *BASIC (Beginners' All-purpose Symbolic Instruction Code), one of the most common computer 'languages'. ASH* and *BASIC* are acronyms, initials pronounced as a single word. The highest stage of evolution for an acronym is that at which it comes to be felt as an independent word; in these circumstances capitals are not required (*radar, laser*).*

Small capitals (a device not easily available to the hand-writer of course) are used mainly as a device for emphasis or, more commonly nowadays, in books of reference to indicate other relevant headwords:

IMITATION . . . the Latin *imitatio*, is a translation of the Gr. *mimesis*. The original connotation of the latter seems to have been dramatic or quasi-dramatic (see MIMESIS). . . . Anything can be imitated, in accordance with the laws of the *genre* one has chosen, and the object, whether fable, fact, or fiction, is tacitly assumed to have

* The various groups that came together in Kent in 1988 and 1989 to oppose the damage that would be done to their communities and environment by the Channel Tunnel and associated construction projects were not equally successful in finding acronyms for themselves: BATTL (Brockley Against The Tunnel Link); Charge (Chunnel Action Residents Group Executive); SHOK (Save the Heart Of Kent); NDRL (North Downs Rail Concern). See *Independent*, 25 February 1989.

more or less the same status as a natural object
(see CLASSICAL POETICS).

Alex Preminger (ed.), *Princeton
Encyclopaedia of Poetry and Poetics*
(Princeton, NJ, 1974)

When dealing with roads a capital is required if the
word is part of the road's name (*Finchley Road,
Wigan Road*), but not otherwise (*Take the Standish
road until you reach the Dog and Partridge*).

If a prefix is hyphenated to a proper noun or
adjective, the noun or adjective should keep its
capital, and the hyphen does not take one: *un-
English*, *non-Catholics*, *pro-Russian*; however,
Nonconformist (in its religious sense only) is written
as one, capitalised word. In the titles of organis-
ations and literary works both prefix and the word
to which it is attached must be capitalised: *The Anti-
Death League*.

Variation of upper- and lower-case letters can
deftly make a point to a reader that would be more
laboured in speech:

British patriotism in its overt form is conservative,
even Conservative.

New Statesman and Society, 21 November 1988

Alternatively, capitals may suggest importance,
loudness or violence, as in these examples from
Dickens and Thackeray:

'At such times as when your sister is on the

Rampage, Pip,' Joe sank his voice to a whisper and glanced at the door, 'candour compels fur to admit that she is a Buster.'

Joe pronounced this word, as if it began with at least twelve capital B's.

Charles Dickens,
Great Expectations (1861) ch. 7

'MISS JEMIMA!' exclaimed Miss Pinkerton, in the largest capitals.

William Thackeray,
Vanity Fair (1848) ch. 1

ITALICS

> . . . *the concluding ten lines, except the last couplet but one, which I distinguish by the Italick character.*
> James Boswell, *Life of Johnson* (1791),
> February 1766

In addition to capitals and small capitals the example taken from the *Princeton Encyclopaedia of Poetry and Poetics* used another device – indeed the most common in printing – to give emphasis: italics. Some people go to the pointless labour of italicising their handwriting, when they might more easily underline whatever would appear italicised in print; italic (originally *Italic*) writing differs from roman (originally *Roman*) by being lighter and sloping to the right. It is so called because it was designed and first used by Aldus Manutius (see p. 14).

Italics may be used to draw attention to something significant:

> The nature of alliteration is evident in Pope's line '*A*pt *a*lliteration's *a*rtful *a*id'.

One simple use of italic is to give visual emphasis to an item that, if spoken, would receive a vocal emphasis:

> 'What *can* you mean by talking this way to *me*?' thundered Heathcliff with savage vehemence.
>
> Emily Brontë,
> *Wuthering Heights* (1847) ch. 3

This is a use which quickly grows tiresome if overdone. Philip Howard has suggested that 'there should be a typeface called Ironics, possibly italics leaning backwards, to indicate to the reader that a joke is being attempted'.[2] A related use, to which the same caution applies, is that of suggesting an item's importance: 'And the greatest of these is *Charity*'. Such uses are often found in antithetical constructions: '*you* say "ee-ther", *I* say "eye-ther".' In all three cases a sensitive writer will think first of achieving an effect by re-ordering the sentence rather than lazily rely on italics. Italic type is useful also in avoiding the momentary confusion caused here: 'He . . . has written two well-known and disturbing books, urging new *mores* . . . .'[3]

The more legitimate uses of italics are as follows. They may be used to single out a word because of its conscious slanginess or because it is foreign and un-anglicised:

> He wore his *fin de siècle Weltschmerz* and *accidia* with a most engaging *panache* and *hauteur*.
> Malcolm Bradbury,
> *The History Man* (1975) ch. 4

When, as throughout this book, words and phrases are quoted not for what they mean but as instances or examples, or as items for discussion, they may be italicised:

> Only the weak will give in to the modern misuse of *hopefully*.

> *Grim* and *grime* have no etymological connection.

Very occasionally, though it is not much to be encouraged, a writer may use italics to indicate the use of quotation or of direct speech:

> With a noisy *hurrah!* they were off into the night.

In all these instances, where a passage being printed in italics contains a word or phrase that would ordinarily – by reason of its foreignness or because it was being quoted – be printed in italic there will be a need to reverse the usual pattern and use roman type for emphasis:

> *The influx of foreign words into English is a continuing*

phenomenon – as witness tinnie, splash-down *and*
rain check – *not just a part of its past.*

The use of italics with the titles of published works
has been discussed above (see p. 138).

In a limited way italics can be used for emphases
of contrast (but not too often): it is not the *amount*
but the *quality* of work that counts.

Italics are used also with foreign expressions that
have not become anglicised. Assimilation occurs at
differing rates, but here is a guide-list of expressions
which do and do not require italics. These expressions should be underlined or printed in italic:

ab extra, ab origine, ad hoc, ad nauseam, ad valorem,
affaire (de coeur), aficionado, a fortiori, aide-mémoire
(plural *aides-mémoire*), *alumnus* (equally *alumni,*
alumna, alumnae), *amende honorable, amour propre,*
ancien régime, anglice, Angst, à propos, arriviste,
au courant, au fond, au revoir, bête noire, bêtise,
bonhomie, bon mot, bon ton, brouhaha, carte blanche,
casus belli, ceteris paribus, chef-d'oeuvre, chevaux de
frise, chez, con amore (but not in music), *coup de*
grâce, coup de main, coup d'état, coup d'oeil, crime
passionel, démarche, demi-mondaine, demi-monde,
demi-pension, de quoi vivre, de rigueur, déshabillé(e),
distrait(e), dolce far niente, double entendre, echt,
édition de luxe, élan, élan vital, en bloc, en déshabille,
en fête, en masse, en passant, en rapport, en route,
entente cordiale, esprit de corps, ex cathedra, ex officiis,
ex parte (but not in legal parlance: 'an ex-parte

statement'), *facile princeps, factum est, fait accompli, felo de se, frisson, garçon, glasnost, grand monde, habitué(e), hoi polloi, hors concours, hors de combat, idée fixe, idée reçue, imprimis, in propria persona, in situ, in vitro, in vivo, jeu d'esprit, jeunesse dorée, joie de vivre, laissez faire, laissez passer, lapsus linguae, lèse-majesté, magnum opus, memento mori, métier, mise-en-page, mise-en-scène, modus operandi, modus vivendi, mores, more suo, multum in parvo, naïveté, nemine contradicente, ne plus ultra, noblesse oblige, nolens volens, nom de plume, non est, nouveau riche, nouvelle vague, obiter dicta, objet d'art, outré, par excellence, pari passu, per centum, per contra, perestroika, per se, piano nobile, pièce de resistance, pied-a-terre, post mortem* (adv.), *pro tempore, raison d'être, rapprochement, rara avis, réchauffé, réclame, répétiteur, risqué, roman à clef, sans cérémonie, savoir-faire, sensu stricto, sine anno, sine die, sine qua non, sotto voce, sub rosa, succès d'estime, succès de scandale, tabula rasa, tour de force, tour d'horizon, tout court, trompe l'oeil, ultra vires, viv-à-vis, Weltanschauung, Weltschmerz, Zeitgeist.*

These expressions need not be underlined and should be printed in roman (accents are omitted where this is the usual practice in English texts):

aide de camp (*plural* aides de camp), alias, a posteriori, a priori, apropos, attaché, aurora borealis, avant-garde, beau ideal, bizarre, blasé, blitzkrieg, bloc, bona fide, bouillon, bourgeois, bourgeoisie, bric-à-brac, café, canard, cap-à-pie, carte de visite, chargé d'affaires, chatelaine, chiaroscuro, chic, claque, cliché, clique, clientele, communiqué, concierge, confrere, consommé, contretemps, conversazione, cortege, creche, crepe, cul-de-sac, curriculum vitae, debacle, debris, debut, debutant(e), denouement, depot, detour, dilettante, doyen (doyenne), dramatis personae, eclair, eclat, elite, ennui, ensemble, entourage, entree, entrepot, entrepreneur, ersatz, espresso, ex officio (*adv.*), ex-officio (*adj.*), extempore, fête, fiancé(e), flair, fleur-de-lis (or *lys*), foyer, fracas, furore, gamin(e), gendarme, genre, gratis, habeas corpus, hors-d'oeuvre, impresario, imprimatur, in camera, incommunicado, kamikaze, lacuna, leitmotiv (*or* -motif), levee, literati, literatus, litterateur, matinee, mêlée, menage, milieu, motif, naive, née, nuance, obit (*noun*), papier mâché, parvenu, passe-partout, paté, patois, per annum, per capita, per caput, per cent, poste restante, post mortem (*noun;* hyphened when *adj.*), pot-pourri, précis, prie-dieu, prima donna, prima facie (*adv.;* hyphenated when *adj.*), procès-verbal, pro forma, pro rata, protégé, quiche, raconteur, rapport, recherché, reconnaissance, regime, résumé, reveille, role, sang-froid, savant, seance, seriatim, soirée, soufflé, status quo, subpoena, terra firma, terrine, tête-à-tête, vade mecum, verbatim, versus, via, vice versa, virtuoso, visa, viva voce, volte-face, wagon-lit.

PARAGRAPH

The last major item we have to consider in the presentation of a text is in the repertoire of both the writer for script or typescript and the writer for print. The earlier discussion of the etymology of *paragraph* (p. 8) hinted at its function in moving an argument along or introducing a fresh topic. Having that function it shows, perhaps more clearly but certainly no more substantially, the intimate relation between punctuation and effective expression, giving the lie to any notion that punctuation is an 'extra', merely an ornament, a barely necessary frill. Unlike its ancient forebear, modern paragraphing is indented – that is, a chunk is bitten out of the beginning of the first line; a paragraph begins a little way in from the left-hand margin of a text. In printed texts, the space is often that of an em-quad. (A quad is, or rather was, a piece of metal used by printers for spacing, and an em-quad gives a space equivalent to the width of the letter *m*.) The practice recalls the first printers, who followed the early scribes in leaving a space here for the illumination of an initial. Conventionally the first paragraphs of books and chapters are not indented; thereafter every new paragraph is. *Hanging*, or *reverse*, indentation is sometimes used for brief prose quotations, though less often than formerly, and thankfully so, since it looks (to my eyes) quite ugly:

Taken as a whole, therefore, the paragaph gives a certain completeness of conception; running through all the sentences that go to make it up there is a common thread of discourse, round which are grouped relative considerations essential to the matter in hand.[4]

The quotation above is from a work published in 1905. Its advice on paragraphing is none the worse for its date, and may be supplemented by other oldster wisdom that could not be put better:

Between one paragraph and another there is a greater break in the subject than between one sentence and another. The internal arrangement comes under laws that are essentially the same as in a sentence, but on a grander scale. The Paragraph laws are important, not only for their own sake, but also for their bearing on an entire composition. They are the general principles that must regulate the structure of sections, chapters and books. . . . We may adapt an old homely maxim, and say, 'Look to the Paragraphs, and the Discourse will take care of itself'.[5]

In what feels like many years of teaching English to students of various ages, it has certainly been my experience that the work is essentially done when a writer has learned how to make first a sentence and then a paragraph; the rest is merely repetition on a greater or lesser scale. The architectonics of the paragraph lie outside our present scope, but guidance for the civilised use of paragraphs may be given in four rules.

1 Keep paragraphs reasonably short. (We cannot all be Henry James, even if we wanted to be, and there are limits to a reader's patience. If a paragraph is in danger of becoming excessively long or cumbersome, find some way – probably with conjunctions – of breaking it down into more manageable units.)

2 Keep paragraphs reasonably long. (We cannot all be Barbara Cartland, even if we wanted to be, although that estimable lady attributes part of her undoubted publishing success to the fact that no paragraph in her books is ever more than six lines long. Our tabloid press often works to even tighter limits.)

3 Keep it varied. Toss in the odd one-sentence paragraph. (More oldster advice: 'Many writers introduce the subject of a chapter, or sum its results, in a sentence-paragraph, thereby focussing attention on the main position'.[6])

4 'Only connect.' (Whatever you are writing, your paragraphs should hang together in a manner that is coherent, logical and natural.) Beginners should check that they are doing it right by relying on conjunctival props such as *moreover, however, furthermore, on the other hand*. As with

learning to walk, one learns eventually to go solo, but at any level of development there is no shame in re-turning to them when the going gets rough.

In this, as in all other matters of punctuation and of good writing generally, there is much profit to be had from reading, from absorbing the lessons that lie in the work of those who have been at it longer.

BRACE (OR VINCULUM)

Both terms are used for the curved upright line ({ }) that holds a number of items together (Latin *vincire* = to bind). Strictly speaking, this is a brace, and is a form of shorthand:

$$
\left.\begin{array}{l}\text{angel}\\\text{cleric}\\\text{epistle}\end{array}\right\}\text{Latin}\qquad\left.\begin{array}{l}\text{scrap}\\\text{steak}\\\text{ransack}\end{array}\right\}\text{Scandinavian}
$$

In its full form this says,

> *angel, cleric* and *epistle* are words which English has adopted from Latin, whilst *scrap, steak* and *ransack* are Scandinavian in origin.

This is a simple but striking instance of the use of punctuation to ensure clarity. The *vinculum* (properly so called) is now used only in mathematics as a line over two algebraic symbols; as such it is equivalent to a pair of brackets enclosing them. Webster gives this example:

$$a - \overline{b-c} = a - (b-c)$$

OBLIQUE (OR VIRGULE)

Oblique is short for 'oblique line' and is written / . Its older name *virgula* (Latin for 'little rod') shows its origin, and the mark itself was the earliest form of comma (compare modern French *virgule*); another early use was as a hyphen in the division of words. Used now in such formulations as *and/or*, *student/s*, it allows the reader a choice of either or both of the words or phrases thus separated; those with a horror of sexism can destroy the flow of their sentences by using *his/her*, *him/her* in relation to nouns of common gender. In philology it may show the successive stages of a word's etymology: '*uirga* or *virga/virgula* (dim.)/*virgule*'. It is also a device for abbreviation (*a/c* meaning 'account', *i/c* 'in charge', *o/c* 'officer commanding', and, in the days of the old money, *2/6* 'two shillings and sixpence'). It is used also to indicate successive days, dates or years (*Wednesday/Thursday*, *1988/9*); and it can give the date (*31/3/89* – in the United

States the order is month/day/year, so *3/31/89*). The oblique is a very convenient device in such uses as itineraries (see pp. 121–2).

It will be convenient here to give a rag-bag of bits and pieces, mostly used by printers rather than writers. It consists of accents and miscellaneous other marks.

– *macron* (Greek *makros*, neuter *makron* = long): indicates a long vowel (*bālm*).

˘ *breve* (Latin *brevis*, neuter *breve* = short): indicates a short vowel (*băt*).

≍ indicates that the vowel is sometimes long, sometimes short.

´ *acute accent*, as in French *blasé*, where it indicates a short, closed *e*. It is found in a variety of languages in a variety of uses. In Spanish it indicates an irregular stress. In English prosody it is used to mark stressed syllables (*To bé or nót to bé . . .*), though occasionally a grave serves this purpose. In the phonetic transcription of dictionary head-words the stressed syllable is preceded by an acute accent.

`` ` `` *grave accent*, as in French *grève*, where it indicates an open *e*. In Italian it marks an irregular stress. In English it is used (generally in poetic texts) to indicate that the *e* in *-ed* is not silent: thus *despisèd* has three syllables, not two.

`^` *circumflex accent*, as in *fête*, often indicating a missing *s* that is present in its English equivalent (here *feast*). In Ancient Greek ˆ or ˆ or later ¯, over a long vowel indicated a rising–falling tone.

`ؾ` *cedilla*: in French, where a *c* precedes *a*, *o* or *u* and has an *s*-sound (as in *façon*), not a *k*-sound (as in *faculté*), the cedilla is placed under the letter to show this.

`··` *umlaut*: as in German *ä*, *ö* and *ü*, shows a vowel formed by the assimilation of one vowel by a succeeding vowel (*Müller* = *Mueller*; *Göring* = *Goering*), and affects the pronunciation accordingly. In English (where it is called a *diaeresis* or *dieresis*) and French (*tréma*) it is a sign that the second of two successive vowels is to be pronounced, as in *naïve* and (if you must) *coöperate*.

`~` *tilde* (or *swung dash*): used in Spanish to indicate a palatal–nasal sound, as in *señor* (pronounced 'sen-yor'), and in Portuguese to indicate a nasal vowel (*São*).

˅   *haček*: a Slavic, particularly Czech, accent, sometimes called a 'wing', which aspirates the
consonant (*r*, *s*, but usually *c*) over which it is
written, as in *Čapek* (the name of a playwright,
pronounced 'Chapek').

/ ○   are Scandinavian accents with much the effect
of an umlaut. The bar, sometimes called the
'bar-*o*', is found in, for example, the place-
names *Birkerød* and *København* (Copenhagen).
Danes call the accent in *å* the *volle* (or little
round cake); it is sometimes known as the
Swedish (*or* Norwegian) *a*'.

§   *section*: as in '§10: Asterisks', indicates a section
or paragraph within a longer work. Also sometimes used for footnotes.

¶ or *paragraph*. Also sometimes used for footnotes.
ℙ

hash: is tending to supplant both of the pre-
vious marks, particularly in America, where it
is much used for the enumeration of items
(i.e. as an equivalent of 'no.').

&   *ampersand* (that is *and per se and*, or 'and by
itself [makes] and'): a useful symbol, formed
by combining the letters *e* and *t* of Latin *et*
('and').

* † ‡ *asterisk, dagger* and *double dagger* (plus section and paragraph signs: see above) may be used (in that order) for footnotes, but if more than a couple of notes are involved it is preferable to use numerals, generally nowadays as superscripts[1]. The asterisk is sometimes used with the same sort of sensational effect as the 'mark of admiration' or to indicate suppressed indecency, expletives deleted (a convention ironically reversed in David Lodge's lapel-button 'Fuck D**k' in *Changing Places*). In works on language an asterisk indicates a non-existent or inadmissible utterance (**He cans sing as well as anyone*, **between you and I*). The dagger indicates obsolete forms or meanings (corresponding to its use before a date to indicate 'died').

Philip Howard says that 'punctuation is the politeness of printers'.[7] However that may be in theory, it is currently the case that many people engaged in publishing are giving punctuation as we have known it some rough handling. We have already mentioned the tendency of many publishers' house styles to make the hyphen an endangered species. New technology is more at home with stops than with fiddly bits and pieces such as colons and semi-colons, and, particularly in journalism, we find a corresponding obsession with short sentences – not just in headlines, where some terseness is an acceptable feature of the form and format, but also in the paragraphs that follow them. The niceties of argument that these marks make possible is *pari passu* often sacrificed for a spurious vividness of presentation in both its visual and logical senses. The most commonly found mark other than the full stop is the dash – which looks AOK on a VDU; the colon and semi-colon have literally been dashed to death. (That joke was first made in 1829, and is getting less funny all the time.) For all the technical advances, there is no guaranteed progress in clarity and effectiveness of expression, as is evident from many recent instances, including those found in the 'quality' press. How the soulless rigidities of computerised typesetting may destroy the sense of a passage is evident in the following examples – all from publications which should know better:

lives-

tock

Some-

rset Maugham

unfashiona-

ble

the obvious iniq-

uity of it all.[8]

You don't have to go out looking for further examples: they come through the letter-box every morning.

Caxton's successor Robert Stephens (1503–59) had an unfixed system to work with. That each of his editions of the Greek Testament had a different pointing indicates not his ineptitude or primitiveness, but a touching longing to make the editions faultless: how many modern publishers would, like Stephens, exhibit their proofs in a public place and reward readers who spotted typographical errors?

5

The Art of Punctuation

Punctuation is, first, a system. It has rules. It is, however, unlike the orthographic system, which is quite clear on which spellings are admissible in polite society and which are not; some are right and some are wrong – period. With punctuation too there are some procedures which must be observed *de rigueur*, and not to observe them would be wrong, incorrect, erroneous, inadmissible; the practice of starting a sentence with a capital letter and ending it with a full stop is a case in point. Where the punctuation and orthographic systems differ, however, is that with punctuation there is some leeway for personal discretion, scope for individual preferences and private tastes. At their worst such preferences and tastes may re-route a text to gibberish or, at the least, give the reader a hard time. On the other hand, used with skill, tact, taste and discernment (all qualities which, in this area of activity, have the reader clearly in view), those preferences and tastes lay upon a text the marks of its writer's personality – or style, if you will – no less surely than do the choice of material, vocabulary and sentence structure. Indeed a writer's sentences have the shape they do only because of the frame which the punctuation makes it possible to build on. Shaky frame – duff sentence; careful, deft, supple frame – sentence (short or long) that does its job. It is in this sense that punctuation is not just a system to be applied with mechanical accuracy, like the rules of calculation or the way to change a plug. Where there is scope for personal interpretation, there are possibilities for skill and taste to show themselves. In this sense punctuation is an art as well as (and here it *does* resemble spelling) a matter of good manners. Joyce ended *Ulysses* with fifty pages that had no punctuation at all. The idea, apparently, was that this showed Molly Bloom's 'stream of consciousness' or some such. The effect is fifty pages of bafflement and bloody hard work for the reader. There are abundant instances in other writers' work to show the private workings of characters' minds in ways that are quite comprehensible to readers – even in the work of writers one doesn't much like. Characters' states of mind have been novelists' stock-in-trade since novels began and – quite apart from the implausible idea that people's thoughts typically move in these formless ways – we have the example of, say, Jane Austen and Henry James (to say nothing of more theatrical performers such as Dickens) to show that what characters are thinking can be vividly rendered without resorting to gibberish – o yes yes yes.

This book ends with a selection of passages which demonstrate a variety of approaches to punctuation. The author does not approve of them all, but it is for the readers to make their own judgements. Some passages have been chosen to illustrate historical points, whilst others were written within living memory and are both a showcase of how the various devices can be put to a variety of uses and an anthology of some fairly smart practice. Read. Learn. Enjoy.

If I speke with tungis of men and of aungels, and I have not charite, I am maad as bras sownynge, or a cymbal tynklynge. And if I have prophecie, and knowe alle mysteries, and al kunnynge, and if I have al feith, so that I meve hillis fro her place, and I have not charite, I am nought. And if I departe alle my godis in to the metis of pore men, and if I bitake my bodi, so that I brenne, and if I have not charite, it profiteth to me no thing.

1 Corinthians 13,
Second Wycliffite Bible (*c.* 1395)

Though I spake with the tonges of men and angels, and yet had no love, I were even as soundynge brasse: or as a tynklynge cymball. And though I coulde prophesy, and understonde all secretes, and all knowledge: yee, yf I had all fayth, so that I coulde move mountayns oute of ther places, and yet had no love, I were nothynge. And though I bestowed all my good-des to fede the poore, and though I gave my body even that I burned, and yet had no love, it profeteth me nothinge.

1 Corinthians 13,
Tyndale's Bible (1525, rev. 1535)

Though I spake with the tonges of men and of angels, and have no love, I am even as sounding brasse, or as a tynklinge cymball. And though I coulde prophesy, and understode all secretes, and all knowledge: yee yf I have all fayth, so that I can move mountayns out of their places, and yet have no love, I am nothynge. And though I bestowe all my goodes to fede the poore, and though I gave my body even that I burned, and yet have no love, it profyteth me nothynge.

1 Corinthians 13,
the Great Bible (1539, rev. 1540)

Though I speake with the tongues of men, and of Angels, and have not charitie, I am as sounding brasse, or as a tinckling cymbal. And though I have prophecie, and understand all secrets, and all knowledge: yea, if I have all faith, so that I can remoove mountaines, and have not charitie, I am nothing. And though I bestow all my goods to feed the poore, and though I give my body

that I should be burned, and have not charitie,
it profiteth me nothing.

1 Corinthians 13, the Bishops' Bible
(1568, rev. 1602)

If I speake with the tonges of men and of Angels,
and have not charitie: I am become as sounding
brasse, or a tinkling cymbal. And if I should
have prophecie, and knew al mysteries, and al
knowledge, and if I should have al faith so
that I could remove mountaines, and have not
charitie, I am nothing. And if I should distribute
al my goods to be meate for the poore, and if I
should deliver my body so that I burne, and have
not charitie, it doth profit me nothing.

1 Corinthians 13,
Douay–Rheims Bible (1582)

Though I speak with the tongues of men and of
angels, and have not charity, I am become as
sounding brass, or a tinkling cymbal. And
though I have the gift of prophecy, and
understand all mysteries, and all knowledge; and
though I have all faith, so that I could remove
mountains, and have no charity, I am nothing.
And though I bestow all my goods to feed the
poor, and though I give my body to be burned,
and have not charity, it profiteth me nothing.

1 Corinthians 13, Authorised Version
(1611)

If I speak in the tongues of men and of angels, but have not love, I am a noisy gong or a clanging cymbal. And if I have prophetic powers, and understand all mysteries and all knowledge, and if I have all faith, so as to remove mountains, but have not love, I am nothing. If I give away all I have, and if I deliver my body to be burned, but have not love, I gain nothing.

1 Corinthians 13,
Revised Standard Version (1953)

And thus as I have learned of them that much knew and little cause had to lie, were these two noble princes, these innocent tender children, born of most royal blood, brought up in great wealth, likely long to live to reign and rule in the realm, by traitorous tyranny taken, deprived of their estate, shortly shut up in prison, and privily slain and murdered, their bodies cast God wot where, by the cruel ambition of their unnatural uncle and his dispiteous tormentors. Which things on every part well pondered, God never gave this world a more notable example, neither in what unsurety standeth this worldly weal, or what mischief worketh the proud enterprise of an high heart, or finally what wretched end ensueth such dispiteous cruelty.

Thomas More, *The History of King Richard III*
(*c*. 1514–18)

But now to my purpose. In every dance, of a most ancient custom, there danceth together a man and a woman, holding each other by the hand or the arm, which betokeneth concord. Now it behoveth the dancers and also the beholders of them to know all qualities incident to a man, and also all qualities to a woman likewise appertaining.

A man in his natural perfection is fierce, hardy, strong in opinion, covetous of glory, desirous of knowledge, appetiting by generation to bring forth his semblable. The good nature of a woman is to be mild, timorous, tractable, benign, of sure remembrance, and shamefast. Divers other qualities of each of them might be found out, but these be most apparent, and for this time sufficient.

Sir Thomas Elyot, The Book Named the Governor (1531)

But now to return where we left. King Henrie aduertised of the proceedings of the Persies, foorthwith gathered about him such power as he might make, and being earnestlie called vpon by the Scot, the earle of March, to make hast and giue battell to his enimies, before their power by delaieng of time should still too much increase, he passed forward with such speed, that he was in sight of his enimies, lieng in camp neere to Shrewesburie, before they were in doubt of anie such thing, for the persies thought that he would

have staied at Burton vpon Trent, till his councell
had come thither to him to giue their aduise
what he were best to doo.

> Raphael Holinshed, *Chronicles of England*,
> 2nd edn (1587)

Embowelled? If thou embowel me today, I'll
give you leave to powder me and eat me too
tomorrow. 'Sblood, 'twas time to counterfeit, or
that hot termagant Scot had paid me, scot and
lot too. Counterfeit? I lie, I am no counterfeit: to
die is to be a counterfeit, for he is but the
counterfeit of a man, who hath not the life of a
man: but to counterfeit dying, when a man
thereby liveth, is to be no counterfeit, but the
true and perfect image of life indeed. The better
part of valour is discretion, in the which better
part I have saved my life.

> William Shakespeare, *Henry IV Part 1*
> (?1598) v.iv.110

Good morrow good Gossip: now by my truly I
am glad to see you in health. I pray you how
doth master *Winchcombe*? What never a great
belly yet? now fie: by my fa your husband is
waxt idle.

Trust mee Gossip (saith mistresse *Winchcombe*)
a great belly comes sooner than a new coate: but
you must consider we have not beene long
married: But truely gossip you are welcome: I

pray you to sit downe, and we will have a morsell
of something by and by.

Nay truely gossip, I cannot stay (quoth shee)
in troth I must be gone: for I did but step in to
see how you did.

Thomas Deloney,
Jack of Newberie (1597) ch. 8

Perchance he for whom this bell tolls may be so
ill as that he knows not it tolls for him; and
perchance I may think myself so much better
than I am, as that they who are about me and
see my state, may have caused it to toll for me,
and I know not that. The church is catholic,
universal; so are all her actions; all that she does
belongs to us all. When she baptizes a child, that
action concerns me, for that child is thereby
connected to that Head which is my Head too,
and engraffed into that body, whereof I am a
member. All mankind is of one author, and is
one volume; when one man dies, one chapter is
not torn out of the book, but translated into a
better language, and every chapter must be
so translated; God employs several translators;
some pieces are translated by age, some by
sickness, some by war, some by justice; but
God's hand is in every translation; and his hand
shall bind up all our scattered leaves again for
that library where every book shall lie open to
one another.

John Donne, 'Meditation XVII' (1624)

They who to states and governors of the Commonwealth direct their speech, High Court of Parliament, or, wanting such access in a private condition, write that which they foresee may advance the public good, I suppose them, as at the beginning of no mean endeavour, not a little altered and moved inwardly in their minds: some with doubt of what will be the success, others with fear of what will be the censure; some with hope, others with confidence of what they have to speak.

John Milton, *Areopagitica* (1644)

Comedy consists, though of low persons, yet of natural actions and characters; I mean such humours, adventures and designs as are to be found and met with in the world. Farce, on the other side, consists of forced humours and unnatural events. Comedy presents us with the imperfections of human nature. Farce entertains us with what is monstrous and chimerical: the one causes laughter in those who can judge of men and manners, by the lively representation of their folly or corruption; the other produces the same effect in those who can judge of neither, and that only by its extravagances. The first works on the judgement and fancy; the latter on the fancy only: there is more of satisfaction in the former kind of laughter, and in the latter more of scorn.

John Dryden,
Preface to *An Evening's Love* (1671)

7 February 1755

My Lord

I have been lately informed, by the proprietor of *The World*, that two papers, in which my Dictionary is recommended to the public, were written by your Lordship. To be so distinguished, is an honour, which, being very little accustomed to favours from the great, I know not well how to receive, or in what terms to acknowledge.

When, upon some slight encouragement, I first visited your Lordship, I was overpowered, like the rest of mankind, by the enchantment of your address; and could not forebear to wish that I might boast myself *Le vainqueur du vainqueur de la terre* – that I might obtain that regard for which I saw the world contending; but I found my attendance so little encouraged, that neither pride nor modesty would suffer me to continue it. When I had once addressed your Lordship in public, I had exhausted all the art of pleasing which a retired and uncourtly scholar can possess. I had done all that I could; and no man is well pleased to have his all neglected, be it ever so little.

Seven years, my Lord, have now past, since I waited in your outward rooms, or was repulsed from your door; during which time I have been pushing on my work through difficulties, of which it is useless to complain, and have brought it at last, to the verge of publication, without one act of assistance, one word of encouragement, or one smile of favour. Such treatment I did not expect, for I never had a Patron before.

The shepherd in Virgil grew at last acquainted with Love, and found him a native of the rocks.

Is not a Patron, my Lord, one who looks with unconcern on a man struggling for life in the water, and, when he has reached ground, encumbers him with help? The notice which you have been pleased to take of my labours, had it been early, had been kind; but it has been delayed till I am indifferent, and cannot enjoy it, till I am solitary, and cannot impart it, till I am known, and do not want it. I hope it is no very cynical asperity not to confess obligations where no benefit has been received, or to be unwilling that the Public should consider me as owing that to a Patron, which Providence has enabled me to do for myself.

Having carried my work thus far with so little obligation to any favourer of learning, I shall not be disappointed though I should conclude it, if less be possible, with less; for I have been long wakened from that dream of hope, in which I once boasted myself with so much exultation, my Lord,

> your Lordship's most humble,
> most obedient servant,
>
> SAM: JOHNSON

Samuel Johnson, letter to Lord Chesterfield, from *Samuel Johnson*, ed. Donald Greene, Oxford Authors (Oxford, 1984) pp. 782–3

On closing this general view of beauty, it naturally occurs, that we should compare it with the sublime; and in this comparison there appears a remarkable contrast. For sublime objects are vast in their dimensions, beautiful ones comparatively small; beauty should be smooth and polished; the great, rugged and negligent; beauty should shun the right line, yet deviate from it insensibly; the great in many cases loves the right line, and when it deviates, it often makes a strong deviation; beauty should not be obscure; the great ought to be dark and gloomy; beauty should be light and delicate; the great ought to be solid and even massive.

Edmund Burke, *The Sublime and the Beautiful*
(?1747–57) pt. III

While he was thus discoursing to me, we heard a voice on the cockpit ladder, pronounce with great vehemence, in a strange dialect, 'The devil and his dam blow me from the top of Mounch-denny, if I go to him before there is something in my belly; – let his nose be as yellow as saffron, or as plue as a pell (look you) or as green as a leek, 'tis all one.' – To this somebody answered, 'So it seems my poor mess-mate must part his cable for want of a little assistance. – His fore-top-sail is loose already; and besides, the doctor ordered you to overhaul him; – but I see you don't mind what your master says.'

Tobias Smollett, *Roderick Random* (1748) ch. 25

My brother, the brave man has to give his Life away. Give it, I advise thee; – thou dost not expect to *sell* thy life in an adequate manner? What price, for example, would content thee? The just price of thy LIFE to thee, – why, God's entire Creation to thyself, the whole Universe of Space, the whole Eternity of Time, and what they hold: that is the price that would content thee; that, and if thou wilt be candid, nothing short of that! It is thy all; and for it thou wouldst have all. Thou art an unreasonable mortal; – or rather thou art a poor *infinite* mortal, who, in thy narrow clay-prison here, *seemest* so unreasonable!

Thomas Carlyle, *Past and Present* (1813)

To say that a thing *must* be, is to admit that it *may not* be. No one, I say, will die for his own calculations; he dies for realities. This is why a literary religion is so little to be depended upon; it looks well in fair weather, but its doctrines are opinions, and, when called to suffer for them, it slips them between its folios, or burns them at its hearth. And this again is the secret of the distrust and raillery with which moralists have been so commonly visited. They say and do not. Why? Because they are contemplating the fitness of things, and they live by the square, when they should be realizing their high maxims in the concrete.

John Henry Newman, *The Tamworth Reading Room* (1841)

'Why she's a liar to the end! Where is she? Not *there* – not in heaven – not perished – where? Oh! you said you cared nothing for my sufferings! And I pray one prayer – I repeat it till my tongue stiffens – Catherine Earnshaw, may you not rest, as long as I am living! You said I killed you – haunt me then! The murdered *do* haunt their murderers. I believe – I know that ghosts *have* wandered on earth. Be with me always – take any form – drive me mad! only *do* not leave me in this abyss, where I cannot find you! Oh God! it is unutterable! I cannot live without my life! I *cannot* live without my soul!'

Emily Brontë, *Wuthering Heights* (1847) ch. 16

That the young man had been visible there just in this position expressed somehow for Strether that, as Maria Gostrey had reported, he had been absent and silent; and our friend drew breath on each landing – the lift, at that hour, having ceased to work – before the implications of the fact. He had been for a week intensely away, away to a distance and alone; but he was more back than ever, and the attitude in which Strether had surprised him was something more than a return – it was clearly a conscious surrender. He had arrived but an hour before, from London, from Lucerne, from Homburg, from no matter where – though the visitor's fancy, on the staircase, liked to fill it out; and after a bath, a talk with Baptiste and a supper of light cold clever

French things, which one could see the remains of there in the circle of the lamp, pretty and ultra-Parisian, he had come into the air again for a smoke, was occupied at the moment of Strether's approach in what might have been called taking up his life afresh. His life, his life!

Henry James, *The Ambassadors* (1903) XII.4

Once in a way, perhaps as often as every eighteen months, an invitation to Sunday afternoon tea at the Ufford would arrive on a postcard addressed in Uncle Giles's neat, constricted handwriting. This private hotel in Bayswater, where he stayed during comparatively rare visits to London, occupied two corner houses in a latent, almost impenetrable region west of the Queen's Road. Not only the battleship-grey colour, but also something at once angular and top-heavy about the block's configuration as a whole, suggested a large vessel moored in the street. Even within, at least on the ground floor, the Ufford conveyed some reminder of life at sea, though certainly of no luxuriously equipped liner; at best one of those superannuated schooners of Conrad's novels, perhaps decorated years before as a rich man's yacht, now tarnished by the years and reduced to ignoble uses like traffic in tourists, pilgrims, or even illegal immigrants; pervaded – to borrow an appropriately Conradian mannerism – with uneasy memories of the strife of men.

That was the feeling the Ufford gave, riding at anchor on the sluggish Bayswater tides.

Anthony Powell,
The Acceptance World (1955) ch. 1

We need, not to return to the last century, but to progress to integrating more people into a balanced agrarian life.

Quoted by Randolph Quirk in
his Introduction to Sidney Greenbaum
and Janet Whitcut, *Longman
Guide to English Usage* (1988)

Our staff have cast off clothing and are eager to show you all they've got.

Quoted ibid.

Buckingham Palace said that 22-year-old Prince Andrew, son of Queen Elizabeth and a Navy helicopter pilot, would sail with the Invincible.

'Peterborough' column, *Daily Telegraph*;
quoted by Robert Burchfield in the
Sunday Times, 5 March 1989, p. G14

6

Historical Instances

Late ninth century. Alfred, translation of Pope Gregory's *Cura Pastoralis*

THIS BOOK IS TO GO TO
WORCESTER

ALFred king commandeth to greet waerferth bishop with his words in loving and friendly wise and i would have you informed that it has often come into my remembrance. what wise men there formerly were among the angle race. both of the sacred orders and the secular and how happy times those were throughout the angle race. and how the kings who had the government of the folk in those days. obeyed god and his messengers and they on the one hand maintained their peace. and their customs. and their authority within their borders while at the same time they spread their territory outwards. and how it then went well with them. both in

war. and in wisdom and likewise the sacred orders. how
earnest they were as well about teaching as about
learning and about all the services. that they owed to
god and how people from abroad. came to this land for
wisdom and instruction and how we now should have
to get them abroad. if we were going to have them; So
clean was it fallen away in the angle race. that there
were very few on this side humber who would know
how to render their services in english or so much as
translate an epistle out of latin into english.

This passage (cited from Skelton, *Modern English
Punctuation*, 1933) is translated from Old English
but follows the capitalisation and punctuation of
the original. Throughout, the dot works as our
comma, the inverted semi-colon (not illustrated;
the curve above the dot has its convexity lying
towards the writer's right hand) as our modern
semi-colon, and the semi-colon as our full stop; it
will be noted that dots occur at stages in the
progression of the thought, and their use therefore
rather resembles that in the so-called heavy system
of punctuation.

1477. Caxton, *Dictes or sayenges of the philosophres*

Here endeth the book named the dictes or sayengis
of the philosophres emprynted by me William
Caxton at Westmestre the yere of our lord. M.
CCCC . Lxxvii. whiche book is late translated out of

Frenshe into englyssh . by the Noble and puissant lord
Lord Antone Erle of Ryuers lord of Scales & of the
ile of Wyght/Defendour and directour of the siege apos-
tolique/for our holy fader the Pope in this Royame of
England and Gouernor of my lord Prynce of Wales

The full stops are in the form of a cross; the virgule
(/) acts as a comma; the hyphen is two slanting
parallel strokes; the initial H is three lines deep.

1499. De Worde, *Mandeville's Travels*

Here begynneth a lytell treatyse or booke named Iohan Mau(n)deuyll knyght born in Englon-
de in the towne of saynt Albone & speketh of the
wayes of the holy londe towarde Iherusalem/&
of marueyles of Ynde & of other dyuerse cou(n)trees.

Hyphens as in Caxton, above; the bracketed letters
are indicated by a stroke over the preceding vowel.

c. 1500. De Worde (?), *Ascensius Declynsons*

Therbe fiue maner pontys [poynts]/and diusio(n)s
most vside with cunnyng men: the which/if they be well
vndersto(n)d both to the reder/ & the herer/ & they
be these: *virgil*/ come/ pare(n)thesis/ playnt poynt/
and interrogatif. A *virgil* is a scle(n)der stryke/
lenynge forward thiswyse/ be tokenynge a lytyl/ short

> rest without any perfetnes yet of sentens: as betwene
> the fiue poyntis a fore rehersid.

Dibdin and Ames, *Typographical Antiquities*, vol. II, p. 204. The unknown author mistakenly calls a colon a 'come'. His virgils are given in Dibdin and Ames as commas.

1521. De Worde, *The Flower of the Ten Commandments*

> Here endeth the boke intytuled ye flou=
> re of ye co(m)mau(n)dementes of god w. many
> examples & auctorytes extracte as well
> of y(e) holy scriptures as of other doctours
> nd good auncyent faders the whiche is
> moche profytable and vtyle vnto all peo=
> ple/ lately translated out of Fre(n)sshe into
> Englysshe Emprynted at London in Fle=
> te strete at the sygne of the sonne by Wyn=
> kyn de Worde. The.xiii.yere of y(e) reygne
> of oure moste naturell souerayne lorde
> kynge Henry y(e) eyght of y(e) name.

The comma is still represented by a virgil and the hyphen by a double stroke. The abbreviations represented by *w.* and *y(e)* are the usual single letter with a small *c* shape above. The abbreviation for *and* (this is true of the previous extracts also) bears no relation to the modern ampersand shown here.

1525. Tyndale's New Testament

> When he saw the people/ he
> went up into a mountaine/ and wen he was sett/
> hys disciples cam unto him/ and he opened his
> mouth/ and taught them sayinge: Blessed are the
> poure in sprete: for thers is the kyngdom of heven.

The initial W is three lines deep.

1530. Skelton, *Magnificence*

Measure.	¶But haue ye not herde say/ that wyll is no skyll
	Take sad dyreccyon and leve this wantonnesse
Lyberte.	¶It is no maystery

This shows superfluous points after the speakers' names and superfluous paragraph signs, but no question mark and no full stops.

1539. The Great Bible

> The Byble in
> Englyshe, that is to say the con-
> tents of all the holy scrypture, bothe
> of y(e) olde andnewe testament, truly
> translated after the veryte of the
> Hebrue and Greke textes, by y(e) dy-

lygent studye of dyuerse excellent
learned men, expert in theforsayde
tonges.

The comma had replaced the virgil by the time of
Coverdale's Bible (1535); the hyphen is still a double
stroke.

c. 1595. Shakespeare, Sonnet 25 (last couplet)

Then happy I, that love and am beloved
Where I may not remove, nor be removed.

This original punctuation is designed to illustrate
metrical effects and to guide the reader in observing
them. A modern editor, by contrast, punctuates to
highlight the grammar and logic of the proposition:

Then happy I, that love and am beloved,
Where I may not remove nor be removed.

1598. John Stow, *A Svrvay of London*

What shoulde I speake of the auncient dayly
exercises in the long bow by Citizens of this
cittie, now almost cleane left of and forsaken. I

ouer passe it: for by the meane of closing in the
common groundes, our Archers for want of roome to
shoote abroade, creepe into bowling Allies, and
ordinary dicing houses nearer home, where they
haue roome enough to hazard their money at unlaw=
full games: where I leaue them to take their plea=
sures.

The double hyphen persists, as do large initial capitals at the start of chapters. The contraction for *n* is still sometimes used. The *W* is modern, not *VV*.

1609. *Shake-speares Sonnets*, Sonnet 2 (opening)

VVhen fortie Winters shall besiege thy brow,
And digge deep trenches in thy beauties field,
Thy youthes proud livery so gaz'd on now,
Wil be a totter'd weed of final worth held.

Each verse begins with a large initial capital and the second letter is an ordinary capital. The author's name is spelt throughout as *Shake-speare*. The possessive apostrophe is still largely unknown.

1623. Shakespeare, *Twelfth Night* (First Folio)

O Mistris mine where are you roming?
O stay and heare, your true loues coming,

That can sing both high and low.
Trip no further prettie sweeting,
Journeys end in louers meeting,
Euery wise mans sonne doth know.

Interpolated songs are in italic. Inverted commas are occasionally used in the period to introduce a quotation (see for example Simpson's *Shakespearian Punctuation*, pp. 101–2); but until the eighteenth century the normal procedure is to set in italic. The exclamation mark has arrived (*O happie faire!*) to be used (according to Jonson) when a sentence is pronounced 'with an admiration'.

1670. John Evelyn, *Sylva*

The *Lime-tree* affects a rich feeding soil;
in such Ground their *growth* will be almost incredible
for speed and spreading. They may be Planted as
big as *ones* Leg; their *Heads* topp'd at about six
foot *bole*; thus it will become (of all other) the
most proper and beautiful for *VValks*, as producing
an upright *Body*, smooth and even *Bark*, ample *Leaf*,
sweet *Blossom*, and a goodly *shade* at distance fof
eighteen or twenty foot.

It is only in italic that *W* is written *VV*.

1678. John Bunyan, *The Pilgrim's Progress*

AS I walk'd through the wilderness of this world,
I lighted on a certain place, where was a Denn; And
I laid me down in that place to sleep: And as I
slept I dreamed a Dream. I dreamed, and behold *I
saw a man clothed with Raggs, standing in a certain
place, with his face from his own House, a Book in
his hand, and a great burden upon his back.* I looked,
and saw him open the Book, and Read therein; and as
he Read, he wept and trembled: and not being able
longer to contain, he brake out with a lamentable
cry; saying, *what shall I do?*

The initial A is two lines deep. There are no
quotation marks; alternate speeches are usually in
italic. The possessive apostrophe is used frequently
but not consistently; thus the title page has *Pilgrim's*
but the running title *Pilgrims*. The elision apostrophe is frequently used: *Knock'd o'th' Head*.

1716. Joseph Addison, *The Free-Holder*, 23 January

As there is no such thing as property under an
arbitrary government, you may learn what was
Muley Ishmael's notion of it from the following
story. Being upon the road amidst his life-
guards, a little before the time of the Ram-feast,
he met one of his *Alcaydes* at the head of his servants,
who were driving a great flock of sheep to market.

The Emperor asked who they were: the *Alcayde*
answered with profound submission, *They are mine,*
O Ishmael, *Son of* Elcherif, *of the line of* Hassan.
Thine! thou son of a cuckold, said this SERVANT
OF THE LORD; *I thought I had been the only pro-*
prietor in this country; upon which he run him
through the body with his launce, and very pious-
ly distributed the sheep among his guards, for the
celebration of the feast.

Dialogue in prose is in italic, but in verse opening
quotation marks are used, thus:

> 'Farewel, says he; the parting sound scarrce fell
> From his faint lips, but she reply's 'Farewel.

The possessive apostrophe is now used in the
modern manner:

> Britain advanc'd, and Europe's Peace Restored
> By SOMERS' counsels, and by NASSAU's Sword.
>
> Addison, *Works* (1721)

Notes

Chapter 1 Points to Note

1   The historical information in what follows is drawn
    in part from these sources: Whitney F. Bolton, *A
    Living Language* (1982); T. F. and M. F. A. Husband,
    Punctuation: its Principles and Practice (1905); B. M. H.
    Strang, *A History of English* (1970); 'Writing', *Encyclo-
    paedia Britannica*, 15th edn (1974).

2   An example of the use of the single dot in Greek,
    probably under the Latin influence, is in a land-
    conveyancing deed on a sixth-century bronze
    tessera found near Croton (and now in Naples).
    It has a forward-looking neatness and simplicity.
    Having begun by invoking God and Fortune, it goes
    on:

   SAOTIS.GIVESTOSIKANIA.THEH

   OUSE. ANDTHEOTHERTHINGSALL

3   Cf. Strang, *A History of English*. There are exceptions

to the Anglo-Saxon norm. When Alfred came to the throne in 871 his dismay at the ignorance of even the clergy led him to undertake many translations from Latin in the hope of kindling the fire of learning. He translated (or paraphrased) Pope Gregory's *Cura Pastoralis*, and his work shows a consistent and systematic use of dots, semi-colons and equivalents of the full stop, to mark the stages of the argument (see Chapter 6). The composition and punctuation of such work exhibit a mind trained in the disciplines of Latin studies with a concern for clear and logical elaboration and expression of ideas.

4 These comments on Shakespeare's punctuation are heavily indebted to Vivian Salmon's introductory essay in *The Oxford Shakespeare*, ed. Stanley Wells and Gary Taylor (1988).

5 Ibid., p. liv.

6 Quoted in Bolton, *A Living Language*, p. 178, as is the Tyndale passage below.

7 William Blades, *Life and Typography of William Caxton*, 2 vols (London and Strasbourg, 1861–3) vol. II, p. 155. Blade says that Caxton uses only the full stop, virgil and colon; in fact he also uses the early (i.e. double) hyphen for divided words, the paragraph sign (¶), a capital (usually) for each new sentence, and other devices.

8 Quoted in Bolton, *A Living Language*, p. 180.

9 H. W. and F. G. Fowler, *The King's English*, 2nd edn, rev. Sir Ernest Gowers (1965).

10 Ibid.

11 Walter Jackson Bate, *John Keats* (Cambridge, Mass., 1963) p. 511.

12 *Annals of the Fine Arts*, 1820, no. 15.

13 Bate, *Keats*, p. 515.

14 Ibid.

15 The transcripts are (a) by George Keats (British Museum); (b) by Charles Wentworth Dilke (in his copy of *Endymion* in the Keats Memorial House, Hampstead); (c) by Charles Armitage Brown (Harvard Keats Collection); (d) by Richard Woodhouse (Harvard Collection).

16 Greene's account of this matter and his related observations are printed in *Johnsonian News Letter*, XLVII, nos 3 and 4 (September–December 1987) pp. 7–9.

17 *Letters of Samuel Johnson*, ed. R. W. Chapman (Oxford, 1952) vol. I, p. viii.

18 Fredson Bowers, *Textual and Literary Criticism* (Cambridge, 1959) pp. 137, 150.

19 *The Yale Edition of the Works of Samuel Johnson*, vol. III, ed. W. J. Bate and Albrecht B. Strauss (New Haven, Conn., 1969) p. xxxix. The printer of the Edinburgh edition (1750–2) 'did not', the Yale editors tell us, 'hesitate to take considerable liberties with the punctuation [of the text of the London edition overseen by Johnson]: he freely changed commas to periods, introduced quotation marks where none are found in the Folio, and the like'. I am indebted to Mr Graham Eyre for views on the current relationship between authors on the one hand and editors and publishers on the other.

20 See Norman Macleod, 'Stylistics and the Ghost Story: Punctuation, Revisions, and Meaning in *The Turn of the Screw*', in John M. Anderson and Norman Macleod (eds), *Edinburgh Studies in the English Language* (Edinburgh, 1988) pp. 133–55. This is an excellent essay that deserves to become widely known.

21 Letter quoted from Robert Kimbrough's Introduction to his edition of *The Turn of the Screw* (New York, 1966).
22 See Macleod, 'Stylistics', *Edinburgh Studies*, p. 135; and E. A. Sheppard, *Henry James and The Turn of the Screw* (Auckland and London, 1974).

Chapter 2   All the Stops and Pretty Whiles

1 Quoted in Eric Partridge, *You Have a Point There* (1953).
2 Quoted in the *Observer*, 23 October 1938.
3 Sir Ralph Richardson, quoted in 'Tynan on Richardson', *Observer Magazine*, 18 December 1977.

Chapter 3   Dashes, Dots and Flying Commas

1 David Lodge, *Small World* (1984) Penguin edn, p. 125; Malcolm Bradbury, *Rates of Exchange* (1983) Arena edn, pp. 141, 198, 230. Most of these examples are taken from an article by Gerry Abbott, 'Mascaraed and Muumuu-ed: The Spelling of Imported Words', *English Today*, IV, no. 2 (April 1988).
2 *Hart's Rules* (1893; 39th edn, 1983) gives fuller lists of such items.
3 Robert Burchfield, *The English Language* (1985) p. 25; Philip Howard, *The State of the Language* (1986) p. 171.
4 Cathy Daniels, Press and Promotions Officer, Hodder and Stoughton, 3 March 1987. The last

examples are quoted from *English Today*, no. 11 (July 1987) p. 22, where they are preceded by a short piece arguing for a trial period of no apostrophes to see if 'civilisation would crumble' in consequence.

5 Quoted in Eric Partridge, *You Have a Point There* (1953) p. 71.
6 *The Citizen of the Word* (collected 1726); quoted from *Collected Works of Oliver Goldsmith*, ed. Arthur Friedman (Oxford, 1966) vol. II, p. 115.
7 *Sunday Times Magazine*, 21 August 1988.
8 *Sunday Times Magazine*, 21 August 1988.
9 The examples quoted are from the Geographia atlas of Manchester; *Independent Magazine*, 5 November 1988, p. 9; *Observer*, 18 December 1988, p. 20.
10 Eric Partridge, *You Have a Point There* (1953) p. 135.
11 As long ago as 1936, H. L. Mencken (*The American Language*, 4th edn) was pointing out how much further things had gone in America:

> The English . . . usually put a comma after the street number of a house, making it, for example, *34, St James's Street*. They insert a comma instead of a period after the hour when giving the time in figures, e.g. 9,27 [is that true?], and omit the *0* when indicating less than ten minutes, e.g. *8,7* instead of *8.07* [ditto]. They do not use the period as the mark of a decimal, but employ a dot at the level of the upper dot of a colon, as in 3·1416. . . . They cling to the hyphen in *to-day*, *to-night* and *to-morrow*; it is fast disappearing in America. They are far more careful than we are to retain the apostrophe in possessive forms of nouns used in combination, e.g. *St Mary's Church, ladies' room*. In geographical names they sometimes use it

and sometimes omit it; in the United States the Geographic Board endeavors to obliterate it, and most American newspapers do so. The English newspapers usually spell out *street, avenue*, etc., print them as separate words, but in the United States they are commonly abbreviated and printed in small letters, and sometimes they are hooked to the preceding proper names with hyphens. (Western Union used to charge *to-day, to-night* and *to-morrow* as two words.)

12 This sentence does not occur in Paul Scott's novel, but is re-worked here for illustrative purposes from the indirect-speech passage from *Staying On* quoted earlier in this section.

Chapter 4   Writer/Printer/Reader

1 G. H. Vallins, *Good English: How to Write It* (1951) p. 106.
2 Philip Howard, *Winged Words* (1988) p. 182.
3 Eric Partridge, *You Have a Point There* (1953) p. 121.
4 T. F. and M. F. A. Husband, *Punctuation: Its Principles and Practice* (1905) p. 55.
5 Alexander Bain, *A Higher English Grammar* (1872), cited by Partridge in *You Have a Point There*, p. 167.
6 Husband and Husband, *Punctuation*, p. 56.
7 Howard, *Winged Words*, p. 155.
8 The examples are from the *Spectator* (16 July 1988) p. 20; the *Times Literary Supplement*, 15 July 1988, p. 78; Howard, *Winged Words*, p. 4; *Observer*, 5 February 1989.

Further Reading

This reading-list is organised in two sections: Section A has books thirty years old and more, while Section B lists current items that are closer to contemporary developments in the subject. Nothing in either list is without interest and value, and I am grateful to them all.

Section A

The books listed here range from the antique, via the old-fashioned, to the merely dated. If they have weaknesses, they are only those visited upon them by the passage of time: all continue to deserve serious attention for the abundant information they contain and for a love of clear English that is matched only by the high standards they set. Readers familiar with punctuation literature will be aware of my indebtedness to these predecessors, who mapped the ground with a clarity that made it sometimes possible to go off in other directions.

Henry Alford, *The Queen's English* (1863).

Alexander Bain, *A Higher English Grammar* (1872).

Henry Beadnell, *Spelling and Punctuation* (1880).

Paul Allardyce, *'Stops': or How to Punctuate* (1884).

T. F. and M. F. A. Husband, *Punctuation: Its Principles and Practice* (1905).

F. Howard Collins, *Authors' and Printers' Dictionary* (1905).

H. W. and F. G. Fowler, *The King's English* (1906).

H. C. Wyld, *A Short History of English* (1914).

H. W. Fowler, *A Dictionary of Modern English Usage* (1926).

Reginald Skelton, *Modern English Punctuation* (1933).

A. C. Baugh, *A History of the English Language* (1935).

Wilfred Whitten and Frank Whitaker, *Good and Bad English* (1936).

G. V. Carey, *Mind the Stop* (1939).

Eric Partridge, *Usage and Abusage* (1947).

Eric Partridge, *English: A Course for Human Beings* (1949), 'Punctuation' (in book I) and 'Advanced Punctuation' (in book II).

G. H. Vallins, *Good English: How to Write It* (1951; rev. 1952).

Eric Partridge, *You Have a Point There* (1953).

G. H. Vallins, *Better English* (1954).

Most of these titles – notably those by the Fowlers – have been reprinted or revised several times; only the first-edition date is given.

Section B

All of the following contain useful material on the history of punctuation and/or (fairly) recent developments in its theory and practice.

Robert Burchfield, *The English Language* (1985).

David Crystal, *The English Language* (1988).

Encyclopaedia Britannica, 15th edn (1974), relevant articles.

H. W. Fowler, *A Dictionary of Modern English Usage*, 2nd edn, rev. Sir Ernest Gowers (1965).

Sidney Greenbaum and Janet Whitcut, *Guide to English Usage* (1988).

Horace Hart, *Hart's Rules for Compositors and Readers* (1893; 39th edn, 1983).

A. S. Hornby *et al.* (eds), *Oxford Advanced Learner's Dictionary of Current English*, 3rd edn (1974, rev. 1980).

Geoffrey Leech *et al.*, *English Grammar for Today* (1982).

Geoffrey Leech and Jan Svartik, *A Communicative Grammar of English* (1975).

Tom McArthur, *The Longman Lexicon of Contemporary English* (1981).

Modern Humanities Research Association, *MHRA*

Style Book, 3rd edn, ed. A. S. Meyney and R. L. Smallwood (Leeds, 1981).

Oxford Dictionary for Writers and Editors (1981).

Eric Partridge, *Usage and Abusage*, rev. edn (1973).

Simeon Potter, *Changing English* (1961).

P. Proctor *et al.* (eds), *Longman Dictionary of Contemporary English*, 4th edn (1978).

Randolph Quirk *et al.*, *A Grammar of Contemporary English* (1972), abridged as *A University Grammar of English* (1973).

B. M. H. Strang, *A History of English* (1950).

E. S. C. Weiner, *The Oxford Miniguide to English Usage* (1983).

Frederick T. Wood, *Current English Usage* (1962), rev. R. H. and L. M. Flavell (1981).

Note also the invaluable quarterly journal *English Today*, published by Cambridge University Press.

Index

Bold figures indicate quoted examples.